Knies

Kries

"Answer at Once"

"Answer at Once"

LETTERS OF MOUNTAIN FAMILIES
IN SHENANDOAH NATIONAL PARK,
1934–1938

Edited by Katrina M. Powell

University of Virginia Press   *Charlottesville and London*

University of Virginia Press
© 2009 by the Rector and Visitors of the University of Virginia
Printed in the United States of America on acid-free paper

First published 2009

9   8   7   6   5   4   3   2   1

LIBRARY OF CONGRESS CATALOGING-IN-PUBLICATION DATA
"Answer at once" : letters of mountain families in Shenandoah National Park, 1934–
1938 / edited by Katrina M. Powell.
    p. cm.
    Includes bibliographical references and index.
    ISBN 978-0-8139-2853-1 (cloth : alk. paper) — ISBN 978-0-8139-2890-6 (e-book)
    1. Mountain people—Shenandoah River Valley (Va. and W. Va.)—Correspondence.
2. Mountain people—Shenandoah River Valley (Va. and W. Va.)—History—20th century—Sources. 3. Internally displaced persons—Shenandoah River Valley (Va. and W.
Va.)—History—20th century—Sources. 4. Mountain life—Shenandoah River Valley
(Va. and W. Va.)—Sources. 5. Shenandoah River Valley (Va. and W. Va.)—History—
20th century—Sources. 6. Shenandoah National Park (Va.)—History—Sources. I.
Powell, Katrina M., 1967–
F232.S5A46 2010
305.9'0691409227559—dc22

                                                                            2009012448

To Stacy Quinton Powell, 1962–2005

Sure, cried the tenant men, but it's our land. We measured it and broke it up. We were born on it, and we got killed on it, died on it. Even if it's no good, it's still ours. That's what makes it ours—being born on it, working it, dying on it. That makes ownership, not a paper with numbers on it.

—John Steinbeck, *The Grapes of Wrath*, 1939

Contents

Foreword

In March 1937, Teeny Florence Corbin Nicholson wrote to Shenandoah National Park ranger Taylor Hoskins requesting his help in settling a local dispute. Nicholson informed Hoskins that her neighbors were repeatedly milking her cows and stealing her milk. "They done my cows bad last year," she wrote. "They would milk them and take thire bells off and pull thire tails and made other threats." She asked the park ranger to move her neighbors as soon as possible, but worried about possible retaliation she asked that he not mention her letter to anyone. "Because if he knew it no telling what kind of private injure he would do," she warned. In closing, Nicholson also asked Hoskins to have her house "fix up" as soon as he could, "for it is in sorely bad shape," and she requested he remember her to his wife.

The notion of a private individual requesting assistance from a federal employee in dealing with a neighborly dispute may seem unusual at first glance. But letters such as Nicholson's were quite commonplace in the Blue Ridge Mountains of Virginia during the 1930s. On December 26, 1935, Secretary of the Interior Harold Ickes officially accepted 176,429 acres from the Commonwealth of Virginia for the creation of Shenandoah National Park. But one enormous hurdle remained: nearly 350 families still resided on their former land within the park boundaries (approximately 150 families had already relocated). Between 1935 and 1937, in the midst of the Great Depression, all these families were forced to leave their homes behind, to begin their lives anew in the valleys below the Blue Ridge. But in the interim, many of them called on the National Park Service to settle disputes and provide assistance as they struggled with the transition.

Katrina M. Powell's first book, *The Anguish of Displacement: The Politics of Literacy in the Letters of Mountain Families in Shenandoah National Park*, provides a masterful account of how the residents crafted their own identities—indeed how they resisted an increasingly powerful bureaucracy—through the art of letter writing. Using their words, she explores the ways in which correspondence served as a political *and* personal response to the creation of the park. Her treatment of the letters reveals people who were not simply victims but actors on their own behalf.

I was fortunate to meet Katrina Powell in the summer of 2001 when I was working in the archives as the park historian. Thanks to the dedication of former park cultural resource specialist Reed L. Engle, a new archives facility had recently been completed and opened to the public. Several descendants of families who had been displaced requested copies of their families' correspondences and land records, but Powell was the first researcher to examine systematically the archive's collection of nearly three hundred personal letters. Never before have these letters been published in their entirety. Moreover, given the budget cuts that have forced the archives to close its doors since that time, this collection is all the more valuable. Arranged both chronologically and thematically, the letters document the residents' requests for materials, harvesting crops, and extending permits, as well as their calls for the National Park Service to settle disputes. Through *The Anguish of Displacement* and now in *"Answer at Once,"* Powell has recovered the voices of people dispossessed of their land so that a national recreational site might be established.

There is a general impression that the creation of Shenandoah National Park was one of the earliest instances of the government—either state or federal—removing people from their land for the "public good." But displacing people from their homes for the greater good of economic development or "civilization" was not a product of the early twentieth century. Indeed, the United States was in many ways built on the displacement of peoples. Even though African American slaves could not legally hold title to land, they were regularly forced from their homes (and families) when sold into the domestic slave trade—not to mention those who had been forcibly removed from Africa. Native Americans had been forced from their land beginning with European settlement in the early seventeenth century. In the 1830s, the Indian Removal Act forced groups such as the Choctaws, Seminoles, Creeks, and most famously, the Cherokees from their lands in the Southeast to lands west of the Mississippi River. Following the Civil War, the federal government implemented a system of smaller, separate bounded areas—tribal reservations—where the Indians were concentrated, by force when necessary. Between the 1860s and 1890s, numerous tribes

faced the U.S. Army in a series of battles, culminating in the Battle of
Wounded Knee in December 1890. By 1900, the Plains Indians population
had shrunk to just over one hundred thousand. All of this government
action, of course, had been in the name of civilization and progress.

In the wake of the Great Depression and subsequently the New Deal,
white, native-born Americans, albeit primarily those from the poorer
classes, likewise faced displacement in the name of progress and development. At the same moment that families in the Shenandoah were being
displaced, the Tennessee Valley Authority's efforts to improve navigation
and control flood waters necessitated the purchase of private lands and
therefore the removal of families from their homes. The same thing was
happening along the border of Tennessee and North Carolina with the
creation of Great Smoky Mountains National Park. In each of these instances, social workers, the government, and other experts claimed that
removing these families from their homes would improve their physical,
economic, and mental condition (although the primary reason for removal
was clearly the appropriation of private land). And still land confiscation
continued. When the Buffalo River in North Central Arkansas became the
first national river in 1972 under National Park Service management,
many permanent residents were forced to sell their land. In *The Anguish of
Displacement*, Powell has documented still other cases, such as the Fort
Trumball neighborhood of New London, Connecticut, where the government has employed eminent domain to remove individuals and families
from their land.

In so many of these others instances, we have no firsthand accounts of
the people forced from their homes. But thanks to Katrina Powell's extensive research and thorough editorial efforts we can now read the an-
guished, deliberate, and sometimes entertaining letters of those who made
their lives in the Blue Ridge before the establishment of Shenandoah National Park. Her introduction serves as an invaluable guide to these letters.
Her discussions of genre, of narrative, and of the rhetoric employed by the
residents situate the collection amid a framework of social, political, and
economic dislocation in the 1930s. This collection will thus appeal to a
much broader audience than readers concerned only with the creation of
Shenandoah National Park. Anyone interested in the topics of natural
preservation, the consequences of eminent domain, or the uses of literacy

as a tool of resistance will find these letters especially enlightening. In *"Answer at Once,"* Powell provides us with crucial personal responses that will serve to make this collection an indispensable work in the study of New Deal America and the numerous instances of displacement throughout U.S. history.

Caroline E. Janney
Purdue University
West Lafayette, Indiana
October 2008

Preface

The letters that are reproduced in this book are located in a small archive at Shenandoah National Park Headquarters in Luray, Virginia. I first began studying these letters in 2001, when the archives were briefly open to the public. However, my journey through Shenandoah National Park began about thirty-five years ago when my father took my mother, my sister, and me hiking through Weakley Hollow to White Oak Canyon. Growing up in Madison County (one of the counties that contributed land to the park), I often hiked in the park, picnicked at Big Meadows, and walked up the fire road to Hoover Camp (officially called Camp Rapidan). I have found solace in the park. I have seen an owl and a flock of grouse there, been lost among the stinging nettles, found a deep and lasting relationship with my parents, tested my future husband's resolve, and watched as my nieces and son delight in skipping rocks in Cedar Run. My memories of growing up are filled with walking sticks, lost keys, iced-over waterfalls, bears in trees, and daydreams while sitting on the jagged rocks of Old Rag Mountain gazing at the land below. But my childhood memories are also filled with stories I heard about the park, stories about the people who lived there who were forced to leave their homes so that the park could be a "natural" place for tourists and hikers. There is a palpable tension in the park. Within its beautiful landscape lie the (often) hidden stories of the people who did not walk the mountains as tourists or drive Skyline Drive for leisure. They walked several miles to the general store or the doctor. They walked behind plows removing rocks to plant small crops for their families or to barter with neighbors. They walked to the mountain resort, Skyland, to work as handymen or chambermaids or cooks. They rode horses to town to conduct business. Eventually, they walked or rode or were driven in Civilian Conservation Corps trucks out of their homes, out of the park, away from the lives they and their ancestors had known in the mountains.

The letters collected here represent the nearly three hundred letters written by some of the families who once lived in Shenandoah National

Park. Not all the families who were forced to leave wrote letters. The ones who did were caught in a brief transition period, between 1934 and 1938, when they still lived in their homes but the state owned their property and was in the process of donating it to the National Park Service. When I first encountered these letters almost ten years ago, I was struck by their contents. I ask readers of this collection to look deeply at the rhetorical sophistication of the letters, to see the stories implicit in them, the pride in them. Although some of these letters may contain phonetically spelled words or syntax that does not follow Standard American English, these same letters demonstrate the writers' veracity of spirit, an assumption that the subject of their letter—indeed, their very persons—deserved an answer from the government official to whom they wrote. As I read the requests made within the letters, I recognized not only their importance for understanding the history of the region and of Shenandoah National Park but also their significance in understanding the ways that literacy can play an enormous part in making it possible for a considerable number of families to be displaced from their homes.

In my first book, *The Anguish of Displacement: The Politics of Literacy in the Letters of Mountain Families in Shenandoah National Park* (University of Virginia Press, 2007), I highlight a few of the letters collected here. *The Anguish of Displacement* examines how social, political, and educational stereotypes about mountain residents played a role in making possible the displacement of such a large group of people. In that book, which excerpts approximately thirty of the three-hundred-letter collection, I argue that the letters illustrate the ways that mountain residents resisted those stereotypes by asserting their identities and demanding their rights.

This collection, *"Answer at Once": Letters of Mountain Families in Shenandoah National Park, 1934–1938,* acts as a companion volume to *The Anguish of Displacement.* With the full text of more than half the archived letters, readers can see more fully many of the ways that mountain residents resisted not only displacement but also the ways that other people represented them. The goal of this project, as was the case in *The Anguish of Displacement,* is to highlight the nature of the letters, including the ways that the people in power "saw" the people who wrote letters and the ways that residents countered the stereotypes assumed about them. My primary interest is in the ways the letters reflect sophisticated rhetorical skills, even if surface grammatical skills reveal little formal education. The goal therefore is not to provide a comprehensive history of the park (which has been done by others) but rather to use the full text of these important and engaging letters as a supplement to that history; indeed, the letters show how calling the families "marginally literate" and making assumptions about them resulted in their very displacement. This collection counters those assumptions. The letters published here provide a rich and untold story about the lives of families as their displacements loomed. As with the first book, I am indebted to the descendants of the letter writers for this willingness to share their families' histories.

As readers examine these letters, questions about who these people were, what happened to them, and what became of their families will inevitably arise. What this collection reveals is that there are many more stories to be told. There are more and similar letters in the Roosevelt papers at the National Archives, in Washington, D.C., and in the Virginia Library in Richmond, Virginia. Due to lack of resources, the SNP Archives are no longer open, and therefore access to the original letters is extremely rare. My hope is that this collection will elicit more questions and that family genealogists, scholars, and historians will continue to fill in the gaps of the untold stories of the people who once lived in Shenandoah National Park.

Acknowledgments

This work could not have been completed without the support and expertise of many people. My thanks to Karen Beck-Herzog, Reed Engle, and Kandace Muller of Shenandoah National Park. Thanks to Caroline E. Janney for expertise and support. Thanks to the Virginia Tech Department of English and College of Liberal Arts and Human Sciences for resources and time to complete the research. Thank you to Ashley Patriarca for technical assistance in transcribing and editing the letters, and to Megan Fisher for research assistance. A special thanks to Peter Mortensen, a longtime supporter of my work, and two anonymous reviewers for their insightful suggestions in compiling this collection. Thank you to Susan Donaldson for supporting this project from the very beginning stages of *The Anguish of Displacement*. I am grateful to Julie Dickey and Ellen Early for helping me find descendants of the letter writers. I thank the staff at the clerks' offices and historical societies in the counties of Albemarle, Augusta, Greene, Madison, Page, Rappahannock, Rockingham, and Warren. Finally, many thanks to the staff at the University of Virginia Press, in particular Mark Mones, who, for both this collection and for my previous book, provided expertise in guiding me through the process of publication. I am grateful to my editor, Cathie Brettschneider, for encouraging my work and pushing me toward sound research and writing.

This research was made possible by a fellowship from the National Endowment for the Humanities. Any views, conclusions, or recommendations expressed in this book do not necessarily reflect those of the National Foundation for the Humanities.

As always, I owe a great debt to my family. My parents, Mike and Randee Powell, never falter in their faith in me. My sister and her family, Amy, Ray, Hayden, and Cassidee Acors, always keep their home open to me. Marianne Powell-Parker and Henry Boehm continue to be my haven. Fran and Joe Scallorns have become my cherished family.

My husband, Joseph Scallorns, remains my trusted reader, and I am especially appreciative of his always available and sympathetic ear. And finally, to Henry Quinton Scallorns, my son, who tolerates Mama at the computer, only insomuch as he can "work" too.

To the families whose ancestors wrote the letters presented here: thank you for your generosity and support. Without you, this collection would not exist. Thank you to Archie D. Bailey, Daniel M. Bailey, Larry W. Baugher, Mrs. G. Owen Baugher, James D. Blackwell Jr., Kathleen Bowen Simmons, Peggy A. Bowen Swink, Judith Bowers, Carl Preston Breeden, Doris Breeden, Harold D. Breeden, Doris Campbell, Robert W. Caton, Brownie Francis Comer Cave, Lois Cave Hurt, Gary Cliser, Payne Coleman, William Wesley Dodson, Ila Dyer Weaver, Judy Dyer Knighting, Ned Ellerbe, Willis Fincham, Michael Fox, Charles D. Good, James Grandstaff, Hubert Cecil Gray, Sandra Gray, Alessa Hensley, Cathaline Hensley, Goldie D. Helsley, Nancy Hoeg, Wendy W. Hoge, Ruth Janney Hodges, Curtis T. Jenkins, Gladys Marie Jenkins, Margaret J. Jones, Bob Klein, Frederick Knoop, Sue Kratzman, Eva Kyger, Alma Lam Thomas, Janice Lam Whitlock, Patricia Lam Jenkins, Ronald L. Lam Sr., Virginia Twyman Lillard, Joann Mason Fuller, W. Roy Mason, Charles T. Middleton, Margaret Matthews Morris, Nancy Ness, Charles Nicholson, Florence Nicholson Morgan, George Nicholson, Samuel Richard Nicholson, William L. Nicholson, Major Ismail Nuri, Mary Perkins, Gail Pomeroy, Sean Pomeroy, Genevieve Herring Pryor, Jeanette L. Pryor, Carness F. Ramey, Tammy M. Randel, Alice Richards, Beatrice Hundley Saunders, Wilsene Hensley Scott, Dorothy E. Seal, Goldie Seal, Keith Seal, Nellie F. Seale, Vivian Taylor Shackelford, Kenneth Shifflett, Larry Shifflett, Mr. and Mrs. Carroll R. Shifflett, Samuel E. Shifflett, Rodney D. Taylor, Susan Trobough, Clifford E. Weakley, Lisa Weakley, Alma M. Woodward, and Ruth Woodward.

Portions of this book were previously published as "Writing the Geography of the Blue Ridge Mountains: How Displacement Recorded the Land" in *Biography: An Interdisciplinary Quarterly* 25(1) (Winter 2002): 73–94 (© by the Biographical Research Center), and as "Virginia Mountain Women Writing to Government Officials: Letters of Request as Social Participation" in *Women and Literacy: Local and Global Inquiries for a New Century*, ed. Beth Daniell and Peter Mortensen, NCTE-LEA Research Series in Literacy and Composition (New York: Lawrence Erlbaum Associates, 2007), 71–90.

"Answer at Once"

Processes of Displacement and the Development of Shenandoah National Park during 1930s America

Shenandoah National Park (SNP) in the Blue Ridge Mountains of Virginia boasts beautiful hiking trails, waterfalls, and valley vistas. Part of the Appalachian Trail cuts though the park, and the park's one-hundred-mile Skyline Drive connects it to the Great Smoky Mountains National Park via the Blue Ridge Parkway. Campers, hikers, bird watchers, and nature enthusiasts—some one million visitors—come through the park each year.

Many visitors, however, are not aware that families were displaced from their homes in order to form SNP. And many visitors do not know about the long and complicated history of land-ownership conflicts in the region. Several publications available at SNP's two visitor centers tell the story of the park's development. Darwin Lambert's *Undying Past of Shenandoah National Park* details the complex history of the park and land, including the Native American displacement and conflicts among British and colonial American landowners staking claim to the same lands. Anthropologist Charles Perdue and sociologist Nancy Martin-Perdue (authors of *Talk about Trouble*) have produced several scholarly publications that highlight their extensive archival and field research to tell the stories of displaced families from SNP. Indeed, it is their work that has influenced the Park Service's development of the film *The Gift* and the historical Web site http://www.vahistory.org/shenandoah.html, both of which draw attention to the sacrifices families made in order for the park to be created. Archaeologist Audrey Horning has published several articles and a book, *In the Shadow of Ragged Mountain*, which highlight her archaeological

evidence that mountain families were not as isolated as park promoters had
suggested when they lobbied for the park to state and federal officials. And
Park Service historians have produced several online articles and a new
exhibit detailing the park's history in relation to the relocation of families. The new display, located at the Harry F. Byrd Visitor Center at Big
Meadows at Milepost 51, includes many photographs of mountain families
and selected quotations from the letters that residents wrote to park officials as they awaited relocation.

Those letters, stored by park officials and located at the park's archives
in Luray, Virginia, are collected here for the first time in their full text. The
letters are mostly hand-penciled, written on school notepad paper, and
were prompted by the families' removal from their land. With the Commonwealth of Virginia's Public Park Condemnation Act of 1928, the state
surveyed for and acquired three thousand tracts of land that became the
park. The Commonwealth "condemned" the homes of some five hundred
families so that their land could be "donated" to the federal government
and placed under the auspices of the National Park Service (NPS). Families
facing displacement applied for federal homesteads, and many awaited
approval for federally assisted loans to move into homes away from the
mountains in resettlement communities in neighboring counties.[1] Due to
bureaucratic delays, however, many families had to wait for their homesteads to be built. During this period of delay, from about 1934 to 1938,
mountain residents remained in their homes while their land became federal property and while SNP developed around them. Some of the residents awaited homesteads, and some, mostly tenant farmers, remained in
the park as long as they could while other agencies such as the Department
of Public Welfare assisted them in finding alternative housing. This waiting period prompted correspondence between residents and National Park
and other government officials, with residents requesting various services,
building materials, clarification of regulations, and harvests. The collection
of nearly three hundred letters, which was recently made public at the
park's archives, depicts a complex relationship between the people and the
government. The letters document individual stories within broader nar-
ratives about the Virginia mountaineer, adding to and countering what has
often been told about the people of Shenandoah National Park.

As several park histories and newspaper accounts of the time depict,
people were arrested and forcibly removed from their land, the state was

sued, homes were razed to the ground, and families were shaken to the core. This book does not repeat those important histories already written about the park and its displaced families. Rather, it joins them, primarily using the words of the park residents themselves to tell the stories of their displacement. The letters voice the concerns of residents, who "have had virtually no hearing,"[2] and narrate the social, environmental, and political impacts of this substantial regional displacement, which is still felt today as descendants of displaced families continue to work to ensure fair representation of their ancestors and the history of the park.

The conception and development of SNP included complex interactions among regional businesses, local and state governments, and several federal government agencies. After the dedication of the park by President Roosevelt in 1936, the Resettlement Administration, the Homestead Project, the Virginia Department of Public Welfare, and the Virginia State Commission on Conservation and Development (SCCD) worked to manage the removal of more than five hundred families from the area. The letters to government officials asking to clarify rules and to negotiate rights reveal not only the residents' interactions with these officials but also much about their daily lives in the mountains and the tensions among families, providing unique insight into the environmental, social, and cultural history of the park. The purpose of this book is to provide a deeper understanding of the great losses that mountain residents suffered so that the Shenandoah National Park could exist as it does today.

The remainder of this introduction briefly outlines both the history of the park's development and its development within broader historical contexts such as Roosevelt's New Deal and the Progressive Era of social and political reforms. Further context surrounding the letters and their contents is also provided, placing the letters, the letter writers, and their imminent displacement in relation to the overall creation of the park and highlighting the ways that the letters provide unique insights into the complicated and rich stories about the people who once made their homes there.

The National Park Service was created in 1916 by President Woodrow Wilson, but it was in 1907, during Theodore Roosevelt's presidency, that Congress approved the proposal for an eastern national park. The NPS surveyed the country to determine the best sites for wilderness preservation. Many of the national parks founded during this time (for example,

Yellowstone and the Grand Canyon) consisted of land already considered wilderness, but the East Coast was largely developed. Consequently, it was necessary to solicit public opinion about locations for a park. Secretary of the Interior Hubert Work established the Southern Appalachian National Park Committee (SANPC) with congressional approval in 1924 and distributed questionnaires in the eastern region. Several states lobbied for the park, including Virginia, whose prominent business owners, and then-governor Harry F. Byrd, saw a national park as a way for the state of Virginia to progress and as a way to generate funds for road development.[3] Several U.S. states were moving toward industrialization, and Virginians interested in business and politics were concerned about preserving a state they felt was too beautiful to mar with factories.[4] Virginia had established industries such as coal, tobacco, and timber, but a group of wealthy businessmen suggested preserving a small portion of the Virginia landscape for tourism,[5] based on a tradition of respect for the land and state,[6] but also because they saw it as a lucrative business opportunity.[7] In order to promote the park to other Virginians and to Congress, early promoters described the area as unspoiled, highlighting the beauty of the mountains and largely ignoring (or not disclosing) the fact that a significant number of people lived there.

In 1924, Shenandoah Valley, Inc., was formed to persuade Virginia's public and the federal government to locate its next national park in Virginia.[8] George Pollock, a prominent businessman and owner of the mountain resort Skyland (which is located at the center of the park and which employed several area residents) and a member of this newly formed group, responded to SANPC's questionnaire about possible locations for an eastern park. In his response, he described the area by saying, "There are within this area, of course, a few small mountain farms, of no great value."[9] The Shenandoah National Park Association used similar language in a promotional brochure, stating that the surrounding population desired "the new national park to be located in Virginia's scenic wonderland." The brochure describes the area as having "magnificent waterfalls, rugged cliffs, fine trout streams, stands of original timber."[10] Meant to persuade local communities to support the park, the brochure made minor mention of the people who inhabited the area or what might become of them should a park be approved. The brochure thus misrepresented the diversity of housing and socioeconomic status of the residents living there. It also created a sense that "small mountain farms" were of no value, that the homes themselves and the people living there could easily be moved.

In 1926, Governor Byrd established the State Commission on Conservation and Development in order to control the collection of funds for purchasing the land that would be donated to the NPS.[11] The first chairman of the commission, William Carson, was charged with surveying and appraising the land within the proposed site. This tract-by-tract inspection and survey of properties, conducted in 1932 and 1933, included a census of landowners and residents in the proposed park area.[12] During this time, Virginia officials interviewed mountain families, informing them of the state's intentions to form a national park and trying to persuade residents to sell their land willingly.

During this survey period, rumblings of resistance circulated among people in the eight counties affected by the park's proposed boundaries. As might be expected, many residents did not want to give up their mountain homes, even for a "fair market price." However, organized resistance did not occur or was not successful for several reasons. First, many people living in the mountains were not informed of the park's proposal until much of the decision-making by the state had already occurred. Second, some may not have known their options in resisting government decisions and laws. Third, the park's plan for development, whether purposefully or not, was misrepresented to the people living there. Many were originally told they would be able to remain in their homes while the NPS owned them. This miscommunication was in part due to a change in presidential administration. In the Hoover administration, Secretary of the Interior Ray Lyman Wilbur stated that residents would not be required to move unless they were obstructing park development.[13] In the Roosevelt administration, however, new NPS director Arno Cammerer said in 1934 that all residents *would* have to leave in order for the federal government to accept title to the land.[14] Many residents felt misled when it became clear that they would lose their homes, but by that time the development of the park was well under way.

Before this survey period, Chairman Carson persuaded the commonwealth's legislature to pass a blanket condemnation law so that appraisers could establish fair market value on individual property. Therefore, the Public Park Condemnation Act was passed in the Virginia legislature in the early part of 1928. A final survey proposed some 321,000 acres for the park, land that was then condemned, bought from landowners at a "fair market price," and then "donated" to the federal government.

During the time the survey was conducted, Franklin Delano Roosevelt became president. When he took office in 1933, he promised the country, particularly poor Americans, a "new deal" in recovering from the Great Depression. His federally funded programs under the New Deal included the Work Projects Administration (WPA, earlier called the Works Progress Administration), the Federal Writers Project, and the Civilian Conservation Corps (CCC); these programs provided jobs to many out-of-work Americans. The Appalachian region benefited from these programs, which employed regional people to build the Blue Ridge Parkway[15] and the Skyline Drive within SNP.[16] As with many government programs, however, bureaucracy often hindered real and lasting help, as people continued to be desperate for the "relief" promised by the Federal Emergency Relief Administration and other government aid.

By the time Roosevelt became president and established federal work programs such as the CCC in 1933, development of Skyline Drive was well under way and could be used as a selling point for the kind of work that could be accomplished through Roosevelt's WPA programs. Skyline Drive, which had begun with federal draught-relief funds in 1931 under the Emergency Construction Act, originally began with local workers. In 1933, Roosevelt's CCC workers continued the construction on Skyline Drive and other park projects after its official transfer in 1935, and the CCC hired nearly three hundred men, many of whom were not locals. After the land transfer from Virginia to the federal government in 1935, young men from the areas of Pittsburgh, western Pennsylvania, western Maryland, and Washington, D.C., came to the area to build the Skyline Drive and to raze various homes and outbuildings within the park that were slowly being vacated as people left their homes, either willingly or forcibly.

The letter writers of SNP wrote at the height of the Depression, when writing to government officials was encouraged by the president.[17] According to historian Robert McElvaine, Eleanor and Franklin Roosevelt "made repeated efforts to get citizens to write to them. During his fireside chats, the president often spoke of the mail he received from the public and encouraged others to write," and Mrs. Roosevelt did the same during her radio broadcasts.[18] The president's New Deal was informed by Eleanor Roosevelt's travels around the country to "assess conditions for herself" of the American public.[19] Like the letter writers in SNP, "more than half of those who wrote to the White House were members of the working class. The economic motives for writing the president are easily stated: by early 1933, approximately one-quarter of the nation's workers were without jobs.[20] Many of the people living in SNP were tenant farmers and lived off their land. Like the letters written to the Roosevelts during this time," the SNP letters represent a microcosm of the kinds of issues facing Americans during the Depression. And like the letters written to the Roosevelts, the letters from the mountain residents address issues of overall poverty, lack of work, and health and welfare, particularly about their livelihoods in rural Virginia.

Just before the stock market crash in 1929, Virginia suffered a major blight that killed the chestnut trees that many mountaineers sold for firewood and lumber. The rural economy of Virginia, which consisted primarily of tobacco, corn, and timber, was depressed before the crash of 1929. In the mountain area that was to become the park, many residents subsisted through their small farms, and larger landowners primarily operated apple orchards or produced lumber. Prohibition, together with the blight, prompted some people living in the Virginia mountains to sell moonshine illegally. The *legal* production and selling of liquor before Prohibition had been a major source of cash for some residents.

With the Public Park Condemnation Act of 1928, the Commonwealth of Virginia condemned the homes of, and displaced, families from within eight of its counties in the central part of the state (Albemarle, Augusta, Greene, Madison, Page, Rappahannock, Rockingham, and Warren). The families living in this area of Virginia varied in their socioeconomic standing: some were wealthy orchard owners; others were small-farm owners, tenant farmers, or sharecroppers. Many of the families living in the mountains were white, though there were also several African American landowners in the area.[21]

Although there were several wealthy landowners in the area who owned orchards or lumber mills, many people living in the area raised their own food on small family farms, and of those, some worked for orchard or lumber companies or the Skyland resort and hotel. Small subsistence farms were typical in the region, as "one-third of America's 'self-sufficing' farms" were located in Appalachia, and many of these "families brought in cash incomes of less than $100 a year (equivalent to about $1,000 today)."[22] In

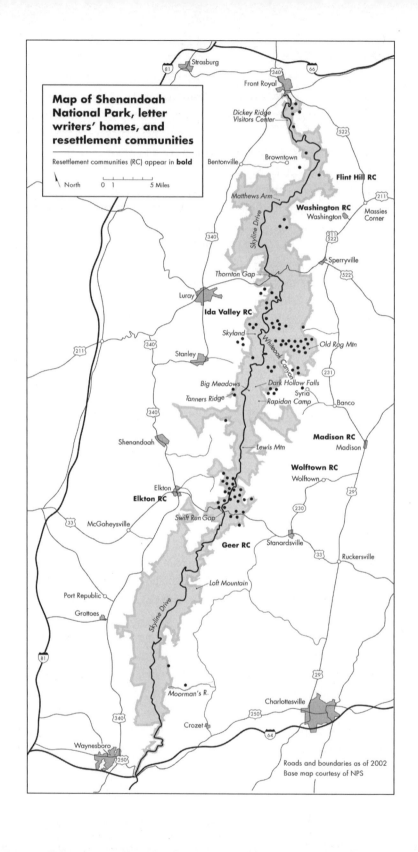

Map of Shenandoah National Park, letter writers' homes, and resettlement communities

Resettlement communities (RC) appear in **bold**

North   0 1   5 Miles

Strasburg
Front Royal
Dickey Ridge Visitors Center
Browntown
Bentonville
Flint Hill RC
Matthews Arm
Washington RC
Washington   Massies Corner
Sperryville
Thornton Gap
Luray
Ida Valley RC
Skyland
Whiteoak Canyon
Old Rag Mtn
Stanley
Big Meadows   Dark Hollow Falls
Syria
Tanners Ridge   Rapidan Camp
Banco
Shenandoah
Madison RC
Lewis Mtn   Madison
Wolftown RC
Wolftown
Elkton
Elkton RC
McGaheysville
Swift Run Gap
Geer RC   Stanardsville
Ruckersville
Loft Mountain
Port Republic
Grottoes
Moorman's R.
Charlottesville
Crozet
Waynesboro

Roads and boundaries as of 2002
Base map courtesy of NPS

the state of Virginia, coal, tobacco, corn, and peanuts were primary sources of revenue, but in the mountainous area that was to become Shenandoah National Park, most families earned small wages in the lumber industry and mostly subsisted from their own small farms.

As a result of the blanket condemnation act in 1928, many wealthier landowners quickly sold their homes to the state at "fair market" price and then left the area to find housing elsewhere. Other families, primarily those who did not own land or who had little means to move, remained within the park's proposed boundaries under a "Special Use Permit," waiting for government assistance through the Resettlement Administration, the Department of Public Welfare, or the Federal Emergency Relief Administration (FERA). Most of these families stayed in the park for one or two years; others remained for as many as five years, extending their permits and continuing to live in their homes as Skyline Drive was built and the park developed around them. It was during this interim period, from about 1934 to 1938, before all people were vacated and most of the homes razed, that families living in the area wrote letters to park and other government officials. These officials and administrators kept meticulous records, saving the letters written to them as well as copies of their responses. Since many

Opposite page: The locations of the landowners' homes are based on *A Database of Shenandoah National Park Land Records*, a publication developed by SNP cultural resource specialist Reed Engle and park historian Caroline E. Janney. That publication includes landowners' tract numbers, the number of acres owned, the price paid by the state of Virginia for their property once the state condemned it, and descriptions of the property and buildings. The publication, however, does not account for the many tenant farmers, squatters, or extended family members of landowners who lived within the park area. Indeed, no systematic record of these residents exists, making it difficult to state the exact number of people displaced from their homes in order to form the park. Therefore, those letter writers living on parkland but not landowners are marked here based on their return addresses or where information based on their landlords was available. Due to the smallness in scale of this map, the placement of names would be mostly unreadable; therefore, locations of letter writers are marked with small dots. Large-scale land survey maps were produced by the National Park Service in the late 1920s and early 1930s and are located at the archives. In addition, Darwin Lambert's *The Undying Past* lists all landowners and all persons living in the park in 1935. However, these maps and sources do not necessarily account for all the families living in or near the park whose livelihoods were affected by its founding.

Spreading apples to dry. Several commercial and small farm orchards were in operation when Shenandoah National Park was formed. Several of the letter writers refer to harvesting apples at the orchards for their "family use" for food during the winter months. (Photo by WPA photographer C. Arthur Rothstein, 1935; Library of Congress, Prints & Photographs Division, FSA-OWI Collection, reproduction number LC-USF34-T01-000361-D DLC; used by permission of Grace Rothstein)

families of means left early in the park's development, the people who wrote letters tended to be those who remained because they had difficulty finding alternative housing or because they were waiting for government homesteads. The letters from both residents and officials illustrate some of what was happening across the country as the United States faced its Great Depression and as local, state, and federal governments developed social programs to attend to people in need.

The Progressive Era of social and educational reforms was under way in Virginia during this time, and several local and federal programs were linked, including SNP, the Resettlement Administration, and the local branches of the Virginia Department of Public Welfare.[23] SNP was not the only project in which NPS and social welfare projects were linked.[24] As for Skyline Drive, the planners of the Blue Ridge Parkway "accentuated job creation as their primary motivation, declaring that the construction of a new scenic highway in the Virginia and North Carolina Blue Ridge had the

SHENANDOAH NATIONAL PARK

NO._____   SPECIAL USE PERMIT

In consideration of his (her) agreement to promptly vacate the premises at the expiration of the authorization hereby granted, and subject to which this authorization is expressly conditioned,_____

of _____(P. O)_____ _____County, Virginia, is hereby

authorized, from_____, 1934, to and until after the harvesting of crops to mature during the growing season of 1934 and in no event after November 1, 1934, to use the buildings occupied and such part of the land as was cultivated by this permittee last year in the above-named national park area; for the purposes of cultivating and harvesting the crops maturing during the growing season of 1934; justification being the protection of the forests from fires and the cultivation of the land until it is determined what use is to be made of this property; subject to the following conditions:

1. Permittee shall exercise this privilege subject to the supervision of the State Commission on Conservation and Development and shall comply with the regulations of the Secretary of the Interior governing the same upon the acceptance by the United States of the area embracing the land in question for park purposes.

2. Use by the permittee of the land covered hereby is subject to the right of the Director of the National Park Service to established trails, roads and other improvements and betterments over, upon, or through said premises, and further to the use by travelers and others of such roads and trails as well as those already existing.

3. No building or other structure shall be erected under this permit and existing buildings and their premises and all appurtenances thereto shall be kept in a safe, sanitary, and sightly condition.

4. Permittee shall dispose of brush and other refuse as required by the State Commission on Conservation and Development or the National Park Service.

5. Permittee shall pay for damage resulting from his use of this property, usual wear and tear excepted.

6. Land not cultivated last year shall remain not cultivated or disturbed in any manner this year.

7. The milk cow or cows owned by the permittee hereunder may be grazed on the land similarly used last year bu on permittee's sole responsibility for damage by or to or loss of such milk cow or cows. However, grazing of cattle will not be allowed in the section of the Park Area between the Lee Highway and the Spottswood Trail and, in the other sections, special authority must be gotten for any grazing other than a family's own milk cow as above indicated.

8. No living timber of any kind may be cut or destroyed.

9. It is understood, however, that the manufacture and (or) sale of liquor either within the park or outside of same as prohibited by law, by permittee or any member of permittee's household or any persons residing on lands leased hereunder, shall antomatically render this permit null and void.

10. This permit may not be transferred or assigned.

11 This permit shall terminate upon the violation of any of the conditions hereof.

12. Permittee, members of his family and his employees shall take all reasonable precautions to prevent forest fires and also shall assist the representatives of the State Commission on Conservation and Development or the National Park Service to extinguish forest fires in the vicinity of any tract which may be used hereunder, and shall assist these representatives in the preservation of good order within the metes and bounds of the park.

13. In consideration of this permit, permittee agrees to prevent fire from originating on said premises, to fight fire voluntarily and free of charge within one mile of his leased habitation, and in event permittee is unable to immediately put out such fires, to notify the representative of the State Commission on Conservation and Development or the National Park Service in charge. Permittee further agrees to fight fires elsewhere voluntarily and free of charge when called upon by the proper authorities.

14. This permit is issued with the express understanding that the same is issued for a temporary period and the authorization under this permit carries no obligation on the State Commission on Conservation and Development or the National Park Service for its renewal or for the continuance of the operation in any matter whatsoever upon its expiration.

The undersigned hereby accepts the above permit and the right to exercise the privileges granted, subject to the terms, covenants, obligations and reservations, expressed or implied, therein.

TWO witnesses to signatures.

_____
                                        Permittee

_____
                Witness
                                Address_____
Address _____

_____
        ENUMERATOR   Witness

Address _____

                        APPROVED:

_____   _____
        William E. Carson   Arno B. Cammerer
CHAIRMAN, State Commission on Conservation and Development   DIRECTOR, National Park Service

Special use permit. Residents who continued to live on their property (or the vacated property of other landowners) during the interim period were required to sign this permit and were expected to follow its instructions or face eviction. Some families remained in park as late as 1939, extending their permits every year and living under federal regulation during that time. (Courtesy of Shenandoah National Park Archives)

potential to improve conditions for people living in Appalachia, an eco-
nomically distressed region."[25] Despite the way the parkways were mar-
keted to benefit locals, however, "the people who provided the land on
which the parkway was built benefited relatively little from the road."[26]
Cultures and traditions were forever changed, accelerating the ways that
mountain residents' lives would change.[27] This important link of public
works projects, New Deal programs such as the CCC, the building of
roadways such as the Skyline Drive, and new social reforms such as public
welfare helps explain the confusing ways that residents were presented
with incoming programs and the implications of those programs for their
relocation. Residents were told conflicting information, probably not with
malice but rather as a consequence of evolving governmental programs
and new communication and bureaucratic networks across agencies.

When residents reacted to this confusion with frustration or resistance
of any kind, the response from officials was often stern admonition for their
not being cooperative. For instance, park superintendent James R. Lassiter
wrote to one resident, "This is to advise that unless you make an effort to
co-operate with her [the social worker] at once or else move out within a
reasonable time unassisted, a writ of eviction will be secured from the
United States Court and you will be put out of the Park." The determina-
tion of a person's "worth" in receiving public assistance was steeped in
Virginia's history of social reform. While public programs for widows'
pensions, relief for the poor, and improved working conditions were being
developed, who "deserved" access to aid became a prevalent question to
state officials.[28] After the Civil War, rhetorics of worth and moral value
permeated the controversies over how much state funding was allocated to
public relief programs.[29] The New Deal greatly affected Virginia's (and the
South's in general) social and welfare policies, but the poor "still had to
practice their dramatic skills as they approached new gatekeepers of relief
in the 'theater of charity.'"[30] As mountain residents determined ways to
obtain the services or assistance they needed, they were forced to respond
to discussions about them from which they were largely excluded. As
residents came in contact with more and more written documents, such as
writs of eviction, from various government representatives, they shaped
their own responses to remedy their immediate needs and certainly to
remedy how officials perceived them.

After it became clear that residents would have to leave their homes, they were then promised that they would be able to live in government-provided homesteads. Some residents were excited about the prospect of living in a "new" home, one made available to them by the government. However, the federal government's Resettlement Administration (RA) had certain eligibility parameters for acquiring homesteads. The homesteads were available only through government-assisted loans. That is, if residents qualified (they withstood multiple interviews by RA home economists to determine their eligibility), they were granted "permission" to incur debt on a resettlement home.[31] The subsistence homestead project, which initially began within the Department of the Interior (where the National Park Service also resides), was eventually taken over by the Resettlement Administration in the U.S. Department of Agriculture. It must be emphasized, however, that many families were not "eligible" for homesteads and were forced to find their own alternative housing.

The federal government's Resettlement Administration (its successor was the Farm Security Administration, which became involved in the process in 1934) assisted relocated residents in obtaining homesteads.[32] With this involvement, a relationship was subsequently established between the Resettlement Administration (part of the Department of Agriculture's Farm Security Administration), the Virginia Department of Public Welfare, and the Park Service. Ferdinand Zerkel, a local valley resident and member of Shenandoah Valley, Inc., later was employed by the Division of Subsistence Homesteads with the Shenandoah Homesteads Project and conducted surveys of mountain residents to determine their eligibility for homesteads. Seven resettlement communities in five of the affected counties were established for eligible displaced families.[33] Many of the letters in this book are addressed to Zerkel as he assisted residents in their moves and access to services. Indeed, Zerkel saw himself as working toward residents' best interests as they figured ways to find alternative housing. His letters to residents are often conciliatory, encouraging residents to seek assistance and stating his desire to help families as he could. For instance, in a September 2, 1936, letter to a resident, Zerkel reestablished the resident's responsibility over an orchard. He said, "the matter of supervision of the distribution of the apples on the several orchards in the Park Area west of the CCC Camp was placed with you again, with a view to your assisting the worthy mountain families and who are prospective homesteaders in getting all the apples they need for their own family use and preventing a scramble and wasting or misuse of the apples by anyone." Zerkel thus described families who were allowed apples "for their own family use" as "worthy" of them. In other words, Zerkel asked the resident to distribute the apples fairly to those who *deserved* them. As many of his letters show, Zerkel saw "deserving" families as those who had been cooperative with the government, who had worked with him and other officials by following rules, signing documents, and responding to government requests positively. Zerkel's letters often instructed residents in this art of worthiness, encouraging them to cooperate so that their requests might be granted.

Whereas Zerkel's letters were often instructive and sympathetic (albeit paternalistic) toward residents, the letters of the park's superintendent, James R. Lassiter, often revealed his frustration at the situation, in which he was compelled to manage a large group of people. When the first CCC camps were established within the park in mid-1933, Lassiter was named the NPS engineer-in-charge of the Shenandoah Project, and he later became SNP's superintendent. As engineer-in-charge, Lassiter supervised all the operations concerning the building of Skyline Drive, the razing of various buildings, and the general "improvements" of the area consistent with the so-called natural landscape.[34] During the first year of Lassiter's position, the state of Virginia still officially owned the land—the National Park Service did not have full authority over the land until late in 1935. So while the park was being developed and residents were slowly moving out of their homes and asking Lassiter for various permissions, Lassiter had to refer residents' requests to then Virginia SCCD chairman Wilbur Hall (Carson's successor). Therefore, some of the letters contained in the park's archives were written to Virginia state officials. This administrative changeover and delay is crucial to understanding the complexity of the park rules and regulations and the contents of many of the residents' letters as they negotiated these rules and regulations. The changeover caused much confusion and frustration as Lassiter and the SCCD apparently managed the people differently. Ultimately Lassiter was given jurisdiction over the land and residents' actions within the park, but this initial stage rendered him powerless in making decisions for residents. The SCCD had jurisdiction but no intention of long-term administration of the various requests and needs of the residents remaining in the park. Therefore, no consistent set of policies or procedures had been established, and much confusion subsequently arose among residents over what was allowed. This confusion often prompted residents to seek authority somewhere else. Therefore, several of the letters in the collection are written to Virginia senators, National Park Service officials, Department of Interior officials, or even the president of the United States as residents sought positive outcomes to their predicaments. Because the federal government would not accept any deeds from the state of Virginia until all residents were accounted for, more than two years of passing decisions back and forth left residents and administrators alike confused and frustrated.

Part of the reason for the delay in transferring land from state to federal government was a pending civil suit against the state of Virginia by mountain resident and wealthy landowner Robert Via. The federal government could not accept title to the deeds until all lawsuits were settled. Via owned a one-hundred-acre apple orchard in Rockingham County, which was included within the park boundary and therefore condemned by the state of Virginia. Via filed a suit with the U.S. Supreme Court on the grounds that condemning a person's land was a violation of that person's constitutional rights. While waiting for resolution in Via's case, the federal government would not accept the deeds from Virginia, and the administration of the park remained in a state of confusion and standstill. Building of the Skyline Drive continued, and willing landowners left, but SNP and state officials were hard-pressed to provide the remaining residents definitive answers to their questions. Some residents, not aware of administrative delays, only knew that their individual requests were often denied for reasons that seemed arbitrary. Via's situation, along with that of prominent business owners who lost property—such as J. Allen Williams, who owned the Panorama Hotel, and Addie Pollock (Skyland owner George Pollock's wife), who owned property at Skyland—illustrates that there were varying degrees of socioeconomic status among residents in the park's boundaries and various attempts at resistance. In addition, residents who were not landowners were not necessarily accounted for at this time.

In 1935, the U.S. Supreme Court refused to hear Via's case, essentially upholding Virginia's condemnation laws.[35] At this time, the federal government accepted deeds from Virginia. The deeds totaled 176,429.8 acres and included land from eight counties in the state. Of the 500 families displaced from their land to form the park, approximately 350 remained during the interim before the land was transferred and their homesteads were made available. During this entire interim period, from approximately 1934 to 1938, several mountain residents, approximately 120 of the 350 remaining, wrote letters to government officials, requesting various permissions and responding to various prompts from the government.

The letters published here include only one side of the correspondence, in order to highlight the residents' stories in their own words. But it should be noted that park officials kept meticulous records, and copies of most of the letters written *to* residents are also housed in the archives at Shenandoah National Park. Many of the letters written by government officials contained clarifications of rules, such as this one by Lassiter on February 19, 1935:

> Dear Sir: I have your letter of February the 16th in which you state that some of the people in your neighborhood are cutting green timber in the Park. If this is being done on the land which you are occupying under a special permit, it is your responsibility as one of the conditions of the permit, to see to it that this practice is stopped and that no more live timber is cut on the property of which you are acting as custodian. Yours very truly, J.R. Lassiter, Engineer-in-Charge

Lassiter's letter places the resident in a curious position. As a permit holder, the resident is supposed to ensure that live timber is not cut (a federal rule of national parks and stated on the special use permit), but Lassiter expected that this resident would also be able to keep others from cutting the timber, to act as an enforcer of those rules, not only to obey the rules himself. It must be noted, however, that this letter was written early in Lassiter's tenure as a park employee. As engineer-in-charge, he did not yet have full authority over the park, though shortly after this letter was written the park was turned over to the NPS. Therefore, in such early cases, he may have instructed residents to settle disputes for themselves, without any intervention on the part of officials. Later, many of the letters written by residents to Lassiter concern disputes they had with their neighbors.

Most of Lassiter's letters were responses to requests made by residents to gather wood, to harvest crops, or to move to vacated buildings. In his November 17, 1936, response to a resident requesting a move, he said,

Reference is made to your letter of November 6 requesting permission to move to the J.R. Nicholson place. I regret that it will be impossible to let you move there. It may be that I can move you to a better house some time in the future. Yours very truly, J.R. Lassiter, Superintendent.

Out of context, this brief reply may seem unfeeling to the letter writer's request. Many of Lassiter's letters are quite brief and do not provide a rationale for his decisions. The letter collection as a whole reveals, however, that Lassiter was often in verbal contact with many residents, and his response letters were often a formality based on conversations that either he or the park rangers had with residents. Probably the reason this letter writer could not move into the J. R. Nicholson house was because it was promised to someone else. Lassiter sometimes does not reveal this reasoning in his written correspondence, presumably because of various tensions among residents or because he or his rangers had communicated these reasons verbally. On the surface though, his denial of the many requests coming through his office seems hard and unkind.[36]

The letters written by Virginia residents contain specificity about the injustices of their treatment during their relocation and the government's responsibility in honoring their requests. Citizens across the country who corresponded with President and Mrs. Roosevelt during this same time period sought help from people who were remote to them; that is, most of the letter writers did not know the Roosevelts. By contrast, the letter writers presented in this book wrote to the park's rangers and the superintendent, people the mountain residents knew firsthand. They expected a response and demanded to be heard. Perhaps the encouragement from the president to write to officials to voice concerns is what prompted Virginians living in the park to write to their local and park officials. Perhaps members of the community encouraged them to do so. Perhaps park officials told them their requests would be considered only if they made written requests, emphasizing the power of the written document. Perhaps they responded in kind when they themselves received written notification from the park or Virginia government (often on typed, onion-skinned paper). Whatever precipitated their letters, they took pencil to paper to be heard. These letters now reveal to us the writers' local lives and provide a political commentary about the government's (mis)handling of the relocation of families.

For the most part, the patterns emerging from the letters include simple requests (for lumber, wood, buildings), advocacy for "nabors," demands for assistance, and resistance to park authority. More significant, the letter writers' values and morals are reflected in the letters—a sense of what is right, a belief in sharing the wealth, a consciousness of using materials wisely, and an awareness of literacy and its power.[37] In short, identities revealed in the letters directly counter those expected of the mountaineer at the time. The letters reveal complicated people with legitimate concerns. Some are polite and apologetic, and some are angry, passionate, sarcastic, and shrewd in their understanding of the situation at hand.

Approximately 20 percent of the letters in the collection were written by women.[38] Although the literacy rate for women was higher than that for men, many of the women living in this area may not have been willing to write to persons in authority, particularly since those authority figures were men. Most of the staff at Shenandoah National Park was male, including administration officials and park rangers. Some women in authority interacted with mountain families, including teachers, missionaries, and welfare agents, but the federal employees who were charged with managing the land and the people living on park land were men. Also, the women's husbands tended to be listed as owners of the land, and perhaps the women did not feel in a position to ask for resources. Finally, several of the letters indicate that women wrote for their husbands and signed their husbands' names. Consequently, the number of letters actually written by women may in fact be higher. The letters that were written by women were generally different from the men's letters in content and length. Many of the women wrote several times, whereas men tended to write only once. Most of the letters written by women were longer and contained more personal information in order to provide a rationale for their requests. Their letters tended to address their values and sense of themselves more often than the ones written by men.

In terms of the physical appearance of the letters, there is a stark difference between those written by mountain residents and those written by government officials. Officials' letters were typed on formally printed government letterhead and contained a sense of authority and propriety.

Many, though not all,[39] of the mountain residents' letters were handwritten, in pencil, on notepad paper. Since the wealthier or more educated residents had either the foresight or the means to leave, by the time SNP took over officially late in 1935, the residents who remained to write letters were those with more limited means and perhaps less education. That is, the residents writing the letters discussed here are not representative of the entire population displaced from the park. On the surface, the language used in some of these letters reflects relatively little education. These surface features, however, in no way detract from the rhetorical power of the letters. Although in some cases the prose of the letters is difficult to decipher, their rhetorical appeals are conventional and point to the "material conditions that produce the tension between literate and rhetorical performance."[40]

Part of the rhetorical sophistication of the letters is evidenced by the formal features consistent in most of them. Nearly all the letters begin with a formal salutation, include a return address, and end with a polite closing, following closely the rules of formal letter writing.[41] In fact, most letters follow very traditional notions of gentility, offering apologies, deferring to the receiver's position of power and previous generosities, and sending kind regards. However, a significant number, nearly a quarter of the three hundred letters, end with "Answer at Once" or some variation of that phrase, such as "Please answer this at once" or "I would like to hear from you at once." Given the significant number of letters that contain gestures of deference, it is interesting that so many letter writers demanded that park officials answer them in a timely manner. This one phrase, "answer at once," counters notions of politeness and demands that the receiver (a government official) respond to the writers' inquiries or requests immediately, highlighting their sense of agency within this relationship in which they had very little power. This expression of agency is significant in understanding the letters as a whole, the residents as a group, and the rhetorical agency that residents exhibited in their letters in general.

As the language and contents of the letters suggest, the written identities of the mountain residents countered what many people assumed (and continue to assume) about them. In both Appalachian and literacy studies, scholars have shown the ways that mountaineers and/or those with little formal education have often been misrepresented by the media and by people with power to influence their lives. Take for instance the photographs of Dorothea Lange and Arthur Rothstein (among others) commissioned by the Federal Writers Project. Their photographs, together with the photographs of Walker Evans, presented a monolithic view of the southerner, the tenant farmer, and Depression Americans in the 1930s. Rothstein's photographs (see pages 10, 52, and 130), taken in Shenandoah National Park in 1935, on the one hand capture an aspect of particular families' lives. Yet they also depict mountaineers in stereotypical fashion. They are represented in ways expected of poor mountain residents: in their work clothes, in front of their unpainted homes, working with apples, with several shoeless children. Although these attributes may very well have been part of these people's lives, the photographs only capture one dimension of who they were. These same photographs were then used against the mountain community as evidence that it was necessary to remove them so that they could have access to a "better" life.

Like many recent scholars in Appalachian studies and literacy studies, I agree that the makeup of the region and people's access to and use of literacy is much more complex than has been historically recognized. The families in SNP "took up literacy as a resource to help them negotiate the experience of being stigmatized as illiterate and manage their relationship with . . . groups both within and outside their community."[42] As I wrote in *The Anguish of Displacement*, "Throughout the history of Appalachia, including the Blue Ridge Mountains of Virginia, people have been made to feel that they must defend their positions, either physically or metaphorically. Resistance and strife continue in contemporary Appalachia, as people are placed in positions where they must defend their identities and their ways of life, taking activist stances against various power structures."[43] The letters discussed here, as acts of resistance, fall into the category of anonymous action, as they were not known to a larger public and ultimately had little effect in resisting relocation. But to characterize the letters as ineffectual would be misleading. Although they did not always incite the desired action from government officials, the letters' rhetorical power with regard to individual and collective agency establishes their rhetorical and symbolic achievement. The letters' legacy and ability to prompt responses in the past *and* in the present speak to their worth in history.[44]

Editorial Note about Transcriptions and Orthography of the Letters

Although the SNP archive in Luray, Virginia, was opened to the public in 2000, it was closed to the public in 2002 due to lack of federal funding. This book, therefore, makes these documents available to the public once again and provides scholarly and historical resources for academics, regional historians, genealogists, and interested family members. More important, as primary documents, these letters tell for the first time a portion of the story of Shenandoah National Park in the mountain families' own words. The letters appear here in their entirety, so that readers can see the full context of the correspondence. There are approximately three hundred letters housed in the SNP archives. Those collected here amount to about half that number and are representative of the kinds of letters archived.[45] In addition, the letters in SNP's archives do not represent all the letters that residents must have written regarding their rights and livelihoods during this time. As some of the contents of the letters written by residents and government officials reveal, some wrote to the SCCD, the governor, the president, the NPS, and other organizations as they sought permission or the granting of their requests from alternative officials. Therefore, more work needs to be done to find further evidence of people writing letters about their lives in SNP.

This book, which is organized chronologically so that the residents' stories of relocation can unfold in their own words, recounts the process of residents' removal from their homes, from the residents' earliest inter-actions with state officials to their final days in the park. The arrangement of the letters chronologically illustrates the sheer volume of the letters coming to the park's administrators. Even in this chronological organization, though, readers will see recurring themes and patterns among the letters, as the section titles indicate. The thematic repetitions across families and communities indicate the ways that families resisted their plight, but not in any systematic or organized manner. The chronological arrangement allows for the chaos and disconnectedness of the time to be revealed. In doing so, this collection of letters speaks to the ways that land and human management, in national parks as well as in other eminent domain cases, occur slowly, piecemeal, and in ways that prevent communities from collective resistance. In this way, the book makes a significant contribution to local and regional history and to contemporary issues of displacement and eminent domain. The letters highlight the issues facing the residents in their displacement, the quality of their lives under the auspices of multiple government agencies, and the negotiation of their rights.

Readers will also probably be interested in a particular family's or individual's story, the outcome of the letter, or what happened to the family after they were forced to leave their home. Based on conversations (including some formal oral histories) with a few of the letter writers' descendants, I found that the stories after their displacements are as rich and diverse as the stories before they were relocated. Where I know some additional information about particular families either through published research, oral histories, or personal correspondence, I have included it in annotations throughout this book. These annotations also include relationships among letter writers, where they owned land or lived in (or near) the park, and how much the state paid residents for their property. This information came in part from research of census data and National Park Service files at the National Archives in Washington, D.C., and its satellite in College Park, Maryland; from records offices and historical societies in each of the eight counties that form the park; from genealogy databases on Ancestry.com and Rootsweb.com; from *A Database of Shenandoah National Park Land Records*, compiled by Reed Engle and Caroline E. Janney; from personal interviews; and from correspondence with descendants of the letter writers.

In transferring the handwritten letters to this typed text, I transcribed them verbatim, leaving all nonstandard uses of English.[46] Several of the writers use nonstandard spelling or syntax, and I have left these as they appear in the letters. This unconventional language use may indicate little formal schooling. For the most part, these deviations from Standard English do not interfere with the message in the letters. In some cases, where spellings are phonetic, I have included a translation in a note. There are several deviations and substitutions that appear across the letters. For instance, several writers use a lower-case *i* for the pronoun *I*. Other substitutions include "dont" for *don't*, "want" for *won't*, "ar" for *are*, "er" for *or*, "sind" for *signed*, "thraught" for *thought*, "fear" for *for*, "thurdy" or "thorite" for *authority*, "at" for *that*, "eny" or "iny" for *any*. Although some deviations occur, residents' writing is remarkably consistent and rhetorically salient.

Indeed, most of the letters follow the general conventions of letter writing, including formal headings, salutations, and closings.[47] The fact that the residents engaged with high-powered government officials despite their informal language skills illustrates the power that written literacy held in their community as they insisted on being heard by those who made decisions about their livelihoods.

For the most part, the letters in the SNP archived collection tended to be addressed to park ranger R. Taylor Hoskins (who later became superintendent), park superintendent James R. Lassiter, or Homesteads Project director Ferdinand Zerkel, with occasional letters addressed (then forwarded to the park for handling) to state senator Harry F. Byrd, National Park Service director Arno Cammerer, and in a few instances, to President Roosevelt. As readers examine the letters, they may be curious about the responses sent to mountain residents regarding their requests. In the interest of space, and in telling the park's story through residents' words, this collection does not include all the responses to the letters. Generally, requests were denied by government officials or handed off to someone else more suited to deal with the request. However, some requests were granted when they fell within park regulations. To be fair, Lassiter (to whom most of the letters were addressed) tried to be equitable in distributing materials or apple harvests, but he was generally strict about following government regulations. Lassiter in particular was limited in granting requests to allow others to occupy vacated homes because of his responsibility to conduct a "historic survey" of all the buildings in the area. Early on in the process, Lassiter and the SCCD allowed some people to cultivate land. However, he did not anticipate how doing so would eventually cause problems with some of the residents (nor did other state and federal officials for that matter). He did not foresee managing a significant number of people in the mountains for a number of years, and granting requests to some and not others set up growing tensions among neighbors (or exacerbated those that already existed). By 1936, he had apparently determined that his granting requests to some residents and not to others would be unfair.

The structure of this book corresponds with the years 1934 through 1938, when most of the letters arrived at SNP. However, one letter was received in 1933, forwarded from Senator Harry F. Byrd's office. Like the letters that were sent to the NPS in Washington, the letters sent to Senator

Byrd's office were often referred to Shenandoah Park officials. Herbert Melanchton Cliser sent such a letter to Senator Byrd, clearly resisting the constitutionality of the park's founding and the taking of his land. Most of the letters in the park's archives are requests for various services, crops, or materials. But Cliser's letter is an example of the resistance that was felt among residents though not written about later because of the inevitability of the condemnation and subsequent "donation" to the federal government. Cliser wrote many letters to government officials and to local newspapers, protesting the taking of his property. In the following letter, Cliser, who owned forty-six acres on tract 183 in Page County, issues a warning to Senator Byrd, telling him that unless his request is granted, he will take up the condemnation case with the Supreme Court. According to Reed Engle, SNP's former cultural resource specialist, Cliser's threats were never realized, though of all the residents in SNP, Cliser was the most vocal about his resistance to and denunciation of the way the residents' lives were handled by state and federal officials. Cliser was eventually paid $4,865 for his property. (See also Cliser's letter of April 28, 1934, and www.clisereviction.blogspot.com for further information about this highly publicized story.)

~~~~

Beahm, Virginia,   August 21, 1933
Hon. Harry F. Bird, U.S. Senator,   Washington, D.C.

My dear Sir:

I have been unable to get anything to do this year on the Sky line Drive I think oweing to my politics there is plenty of work and lots of men in this locality who want employment.

I am asking that better arrangements be made for employment of local men without favor of color, party or race.

My property as well as my neighbors is handicapped from a commercial standpoint by the Shenandoah National Park Condemnation procedure which is void and empty as a gourd.

I never have acquesced to it in any way but have been suffering by it now. I humbly ask for a light job and good wages where I won't be exposed to the weather and where I can be home where I now live at night. Or in other words I must have all that I ask for. Otherwise I will go to court and ask the Judge to set the whole condemnation procedure aside as it conflicts with the Constitution of the U.S. and our Good President will see that its declared void.

I am not making this letter public at all at present it is a matter between you and I and you have only three days to decide I'll expect to hear from you Firday morning the 25 of August or I'll proceed and out she goes.

Respy. HM Cliser
Beahm, Va

Although this direct resistance to the taking of families' homes and property is unusual in the collection of letters, it reveals the underlying tension in many of the letters printed here. The correspondence between mountain residents and government officials tells a unique story about the people displaced from their mountain homes in order to form this national park and tourist attraction. The letters in the collection are diverse: wealthy landowners asked to continue their orchard operations, tenant farmers requested to remain in their current homes another year, and neighbors desperately sought assistance in settling disputes with one another. As they wrote these requests and others, the residents revealed the magnitude of the effects of the displacement process on their lives. These never-before-published letters provide a rare glimpse into the lives of the mountaineers as "condensed autobiographies"[48]—they provide in *their* words an account of how they continued to cope with the challenges of their looming displacement.

Notes

1. The resettlement communities included Ida Valley in Page County, Madison and Wolftown in Madison County, Flint Hill and Washington in Rappahannock County, Geer in Greene County, and Elkton in Rockingham County. While some mountain residents relocated to these resettlement communities, others found their own housing, mostly in neighboring communities. See the map on page 8, which identifies these neighboring and resettlement communities.

2. A. Whisnant, *Super-Scenic Motorway*, 109. Whisnant's extensive history of the Blue Ridge Parkway outlines many of the same political issues, including displacement, land management and acquisition, and design, at work in the development of Shenandoah National Park.

3. Governor Byrd owned twenty-seven acres (Tract 663) in Page County, a tract

that was assessed at $375 in the state's original survey. Byrd's land did not become part of the park.

4. The issues of industrialization and reconstruction in Virginia were similar to those in other southern states recovering from the Civil War.

5. Two related movements occurred in the late nineteenth century, the conservation movement and the tourism movement. See Aron's *Working at Play.*

6. Virginia has a tradition of "honor," for example, Robert E. Lee's sense of being Virginian first and American second. See Wyatt-Brown's discussion of honor, grace, and war in *The Shaping of Southern Culture.*

7. See A. Whisnant's *Super-Scenic Motorway* for a detailed discussion of similar issues concerning the Blue Ridge Parkway. Whisnant's vast history of the parkway parallels many of the issues facing residents and concerned community members in SNP. See also Olson's "In the Public Interest?"

8. See "Administrative History of the Park," on the National Park Service Web site, at www.cr.nps.gov/history/HISNPS/NPSHistory/adminhistory.htm, where there is a complete description of the cast of characters involved in promoting, founding, and developing Shenandoah National Park.

9. See Pollock's "Answer to Government Questionnaire."

10. See Northern Virginia Park Association's "A National Park," 5–6.

11. The SCCD was also charged with establishing Virginia State Parks. At the same time that SNP was being developed, Virginia's first six state parks were also being developed: Seashore, Westmoreland, Staunton River, Douthat, Fairy Stone, and Hungry Mother.

12. These land-tract surveys—which include ownership information, land values, and the amounts paid to landowners—are currently housed in the Shenandoah National Park's Archives.

13. See Engle, "Shenandoah National Park: A Historical Overview," 9.

14. See Horning, *In the Shadow of Ragged Mountain,* 100.

15. See A. Whisnant's *Super-Scenic Motorway,* in which she details the development of the Blue Ridge Parkway, which extends from the southern end of Shenandoah National Park through North Carolina to Great Smoky Mountains National Park. As with SNP, many tourists were unaware of the tensions and conflicts that were involved in building this scenic motorway. Whisnant's book highlights the relationships among key players and stakeholders as the road was designed, land was purchased or placed under easement, and various histories of the area were written. Like *The Anguish of Displacement,* Whisnant's discussion points to the complicated issues surrounding the notion of the "public good" in developing a tourist attraction.

16. See Heinemann's *Depression and New Deal in Virginia,* which covers the history of the federal programs in the state of Virginia, particularly the way that Senator Harry Byrd resisted the New Deal.

17. Many of the letters collected in McElvaine's *Down and Out in the Great Depression* were written during the same years as the letters gathered here.

18. McElvaine, *Down and Out in the Great Depression*, 5.

19. Knepper, *Dear Mrs. Roosevelt*, 5. In this collection, Knepper describes the massive correspondence sent to the First Lady during Roosevelt's presidency. See also Cohen, ed., *Dear Mrs. Roosevelt*.

20. McElvaine, *Down and Out in the Great Depression*, 7.

21. See Engle's "Segregation/Desegregation" and Krutko's "Lewis Mountain." This demographic makeup reflected that of the region after the Civil War. According to 1930 census data, more blacks tended to live in urban areas after the Civil War and during Reconstruction. In 1930, 2,421,851 people lived in the state of Virginia: 26.8 percent were black, and 73.1 percent were white. Between the 1920 and 1930 censuses, blacks steadily migrated from Virginia's rural communities, while whites steadily moved to or remained in rural communities. Approximately 350 landowners were displaced from their homes to form SNP, but none was African American. The original survey for the park did include the land of several African American landowners, but their land did not end up within the final park boundaries. There are no records of African Americans writing letters to the Park Service during this time, but their story is yet another layer of the untold narrative about the history of the region.

22. Straw and Blethen, *High Mountains Rising*, 75.

23. See Link's *A Hard Country and a Lonely Place*, in which he discusses the history of Progressive Era education in Virginia.

24. See A. Whisnant's more detailed discussion about the history of the Blue Ridge Parkway, *Super-Scenic Motorway*, in which she points to the all-too-similar frustrations experienced by landowners along the parkway as divisions of responsibility among government agencies and issues of fairness plagued its development, just as they did with SNP. See also Olson's "In the Public Interest?" in which he says, "the New Deal provided much of the funding for depression-era parkways," although the Skyline Drive "was a legacy of President Herbert Hoover," who believed "that a scenic highway project in the newly created Shenandoah National Park would generate jobs for some Americans" (101).

25. Olson, "In the Public Interest?" 102.

26. Ibid., 112.

27. See Green's introduction to *The New Deal and Beyond*, in which she states that "New Deal agencies compelled southern states to create statewide welfare programs for the first time. Under pressure from such agencies as the Federal Emergency Relief Administration, the states had to hire professional staff, establish systematic reporting procedures, and learn how to calculate family budgets" (x). In addition, the efforts of the women working for the Resettlement Administration "paralleled those of social workers" (xi).

28. See Lassiter's letter dated April 10, 1936. As McElvaine points out, the prevailing attitude in the country at the time was that only people "worthy" of assistance deserved the help of government programs. He says, "Most Americans possessed a belief that such worthy poor should be helped" but that "charity should be

extremely difficult to qualify for and should be handed entirely on the local level. If such precautions were not taken, many feared, relief would undermine self-reliance" (*Down and Out in the Great Depression*, 22).

29. See Green's *This Business of Relief*, in which she discusses the ways that public relief and assistance programs developed in Richmond, Virginia. See also Skocpol's *Protecting Soldiers and Mothers*, in which she discusses the origins of relief programs with widows' pensions during the Civil War.

30. See Green, *This Business of Relief*, 112.

31. Some residents had never paid a mortgage, because they had made their living off their land in the mountains. Consequently, some could not afford their loan payments on their government resettlement homes. Therefore, when they lost their resettlement homes, it was a second blow to them after their original displacement from the park. See the map on page 8, on which the resettlement communities are identified.

32. The Resettlement Administration accepted the proposal of Miriam Sizer that mountain residents living in the park and unable to move of their own financial accord be relocated to homesteads subsidized by the government. See Sizer's "Tabulations."

33. See Heinemann's *Depression and New Deal in Virginia*, in which he explains Virginia's and especially Harry F. Byrd's involvement in establishing the park. However, Byrd was very opposed to the homesteads project, and to many of the New Deal's programs for that matter, because he saw the Resettlement Administration's program as "wasteful and socialistic in orientation" (ibid., 228n. 45). See also Heinemann's *Harry Byrd of Virginia*.

34. See Ethan Carr's *Wilderness by Design*, in which he discusses the notions of park design and development as preservation. During the park's development, residents at SNP were seen as an impairment to the natural environment. Carr's discussion focuses on the tensions between creating and maintaining a wilderness in the national parks while at the same time accommodating visitors to those parks, but he also highlights the ways that the complex interactions of the public, park designers and planners, and landowners today can consist of mutual relationships.

35. See the epilogue for further discussion about the significance of this case to more contemporary issues of displacement and states' condemnation laws.

36. Some of Lassiter's letters were quite curt and revealed his irritation with residents as they either broke rules or drew him into their neighborly disputes. His larger frustration was with the situation, however. As an engineer charged with building Skyline Drive and administering a "natural" park, Lassiter was neither prepared nor trained for the management of people as they remained on their land for a number of years before they were able to relocate. Therefore, some of his letters are seemingly abrupt, especially when the letters written to him include so much personal information and pleading. Indeed, the Campbells' letter to Lassiter, signed "Mrs. Campbell," was fourteen pages long, as she reasoned why she should be able to move to the Nicholson home after it was vacated. Lillie Pearl Nicholson Campbell

wrote several multiple-paged letters to Lassiter. Why Lassiter wrote his response to Mr. Campbell is not clear. It may have been a mistake, or it may have been that he decided to write directly to James Campbell based on speaking to him personally. Several letters signed "Jas Campbell" or "Mr. J.R. Campbell" are in the same handwriting as those signed "Mrs. J.R. Campbell." Therefore, Lassiter may have known that Lillie wrote letters for her husband and decided to write directly to him.

37. According to Lucille Schultz, letter-writing instruction not only taught students "how to write business and social correspondence" but also "inculcat[ed] children with the manners and morals of polite society in 19th century America" ("Letter-Writing Instruction," 110). We can see this sense of manners in some of the letters, but not all. Schultz also suggests that although in some cases letters were an occasion to reflect these classed values, they were also an occasion "for resisting dominant social codes" (111). In addition, "advice books and letter-writers encouraged those aspiring to middle-class status to cultivate an epistolary mastery of the varied occasions of business and domestic life" (Decker, *Epistolary Practices*, 60).

38. As the census data show, the literacy rate for women was higher than for men, and more girls attended school than boys. In 1930, there were 1,872,838 people ages ten and over populating the state of Virginia. Of these, 8.7 percent were illiterate, compared to 11.2 percent in 1920 (*Fifteenth Census*, Table 7, 1146). Of adults (ages twenty-one and over), 12.1 percent of men were illiterate, and 9.5 percent of women were illiterate. The percentage of females ages five to twenty attending school in rural areas was 63.8 percent, and the percentage of males attending school was 61.4 percent (*Fifteenth Census*, Table 6, 1145). In Virginia, as in most of the country, the illiteracy rates decreased among school-age children as public education was implemented and developed. In the eight counties that formed Shenandoah National Park, the literacy rates were similar to the state's, except for the counties that were largely mountainous and rural (Madison, Greene, Rappahannock) and that consequently contributed the most land to the park. See my article "Virginia Women Writing to Government Officials," in which I discuss issues of gender further.

39. Several of the letters were typed by a government office assistant, then forwarded to SNP. In the following chapters, I note which letters were typed from a handwritten letter.

40. I thank the anonymous reader who pointed this out to me in this way.

41. See Schultz's "Letter-Writing Instruction."

42. Donehower, "Rhetorics and Realities," 68. Donehower draws conclusions about a community in western North Carolina. Her discussion focuses on the ways that Appalachian stereotypes and conceptions of literacy have extended to rural communities across the United States.

43. Powell, *The Anguish of Displacement*, 25. For instance, there is a current AIDS activist movement in Appalachia. See Mary K. Anglin, *Women, Power, and Dissent in the Hills of Carolina*. Several working-class women's labor movements have been organized recently and have traditions in Appalachia. See Sally Ward Maggard's "Gender, Race, Place." The 1922 national coal strike is one such instance in which

Appalachians took a definitive stance against powerful businesses. According to Dwight Billings, however, there are other countless anonymous actions that resist the stereotypes of Appalachia. See Billings, introduction to *Confronting Appalachian Stereotypes*, 15.

44. In *The Anguish of Displacement*, I discuss more fully the ways that literacy and Appalachian/mountaineer identities reveal complex negotiations between residents and the government officials holding power over their material lives.

45. Of the approximately three hundred letters contained in the archive, only about half are included here. In some cases I chose not to include letters that were quite short or repetitive. In other cases, I was not able to include certain letters either because I could not find the descendants of the letter writers or because the descendants did not grant permission for the letters to be published. Some of the letter writers who are not included in this volume but whose letters are housed in the Shenandoah National Park Archives include Ella S. Franck, J. A. Jewell, Daisy and Haywood Nicholson, Jack Rosson, and G. A. Sandy.

46. According to Cohen, "the errors in the letters . . . [are] valuable as markers of class and social inequity in Depression America," *Dear Mrs. Roosevelt*, p. 31.

47. Most letters are clearly dated in the headings. For those that were not dated or for which the date is obscured, however, I place them in the section corresponding to when I think they were most likely written based on the letters' content; I indicate these letters in the notes. In some cases where there is not a date provided by the letter writer, I refer to the SNP stamp that indicates when the letter was received.

48. Cohen, *Dear Mrs. Roosevelt*, 17. Cohen describes the letters written to Eleanor Roosevelt this way.

Removing Materials, Collecting Wood, and Requesting Assistance

In 1934, an early year of the park's authority over remaining park residents, only a few letters arrived at the park's office, the first indication of the kinds of letters that would continue to arrive at the Luray office as residents needed more and more assistance and clarification of park regulations. As discussed in the introduction, the majority of the people remaining in the park were awaiting homesteads. As the remaining residents began moving from their homes, they wrote to park officials to request that they be able to remove some of their building and fencing materials so that they might use them to build new homes or outbuildings, either at their homestead locations or at property found independently or by social services. They tried to negotiate the use of these materials rather than have them be wasted. That is, the CCC often razed vacated buildings, which many residents considered a waste when they could put the materials to use. The letters requesting this kind of permission came after many residents were reprimanded for removing the materials without official authorization. Many of the letters therefore contain requests for permission to remove these materials.

Similarly, some residents also wrote to request the removal of dead wood from the park. Because removing green or live timber from park property was strictly forbidden, residents were careful to distinguish that they requested wood that had already fallen and was dead. What had been a common practice within the mountains became illegal once the state and federal governments owned the land. However, if residents wrote asking permission to remove dead wood, depending on the situation, some were granted permission to do so.

A typical mountain home in Virginia eventually razed by the Civilian Conservation Corps. Some buildings of this type were kept as administrative buildings for CCC or the park, but most were destroyed. Pictured in front of the home are William Erastus "Rast" Nicholson, his son Robert, and Park Ranger Gibbs. Rast owned thirty-seven acres in Madison County on tract 5 and was paid $615 by the state after his property was condemned. (Courtesy of Shenandoah National Park Archives)

In addition to the letters that request the removal of materials from various home sites, several letters requesting the intervention of park officials began to arrive during 1934. For instance, on December 29, Teeny Florence Corbin Nicholson wrote, "some one came to my place and robed [*sic*] two windows and some roofing paper. . . . I thought it best to notify you." Nicholson's letter reported what happened but also addressed the park's responsibility to intervene on her behalf. This letter is one of the first to point to the ways the park administration was to become the law enforcement in the area, and people's interactions sometimes required intercession from park officials.

Although the letters of 1934 focus on requesting permissions and assistance, the year begins with Melanchton Cliser, who in his resistance to the park's taking over of land, wrote to President Roosevelt in an attempt to alert him to the "times" landowners were suffering. As emphasized in the introduction, Cliser's letters were unusual, since most letters written by families in the park requested services and did not resist the park, at least not in the direct way that Cliser did.

Beahm, Virginia.   April 28, 1934.

To the President:

Please find enclosed certain Shenandoah National Park papers.

Times are getting only tollerable when a good citizen who has placed
himself under no obligations to be compelled to move or get a permit
from the gentlemen whose signature is fixed to the papers. The representative visited me but I signed nothing.

Respectfully
H. M. Cliser,[1]
Beahm, Va.

1. See also the letter of August 21, 1933 (in the introduction, on pp. 24–25).

May 19, 1934   Swift Run, Va.

Dear Sir;

I received your letter some time ago in regard to the homestead it seems
to be a very fair offer in every way. but I had rather build my own home
if I can get the buildings where I live at a reasonable price. I want to
tear them down and build again in the valley near Elkton they are all old
buildings I don't think they would be much good in the Park. so please let
me know at once whether the buildings is for sale and how the price is. it
is the place T.B. Hensley. owned, on Spottswood trail just above Swift
Run. Va. Yours Truly

Elmer Hensley[1]
Swift Run. Virginia.

1. Elmer Hensley asked to remove the building materials where he lived in order
to build in another location. Many residents made similar requests, seeing the use of
existing materials as more desirable than incurring debt with a government homestead. Thomas B. Hensley, Elmer Hensley's uncle (and Nicholas Wysong Hensley's
brother), owned 220 acres on tract 51 in Rockingham County, for which the state
paid $6,360. In Ferdinand Zerkel's response to Elmer Hensley, he said, "I am send-
ing a copy of your letter to the Hon. William E. Carson, Chairman, State Commission on Conservation and Development, Riverton, Virginia, and a copy of your letter
is sent, also, to Mr. J.R. Lassiter, Engineer in Charge, Shenandoah National Park,

Luray, Virginia. These gentlemen will consider your request and confer on the matter and, if your proposition to purchase these buildings can be considered at this time, you will be advised to that effect by one of them" (May 28, 1934). Zerkel's response was typical of those written to residents, as he forwarded requests to Carson, who had authority at that time, and Lassiter, who eventually had authority over the land and materials. In a later letter, Lassiter wrote to Hensley, "I regret to inform you that it will be impossible to give you the old buildings on the T.B. Hensley place." No explanation is provided. Many letters from Lassiter to residents are similar. See also Hensley's letter dated December 5, 1936.

June 19 1934   Gordonsville Va   star R Box 52

Dear sir

in reply to your letter Rec'd a few days ago: I will not give no 90 day option I will take fifteen Hundred dollars cash if sold in ten days from this date. Conserssion [considering] the tracts my deed calls for 3 different tracts all Joining all in same deed one 65 acres one 21 acres one 14 acres 1 rod and 20 Polls which makes over one Hundred acres if you are intress in Buying you will find it on record in deed Book 82 Page 221 Ja Jewell— several wanted an option on it But I would not take it

Your truly J.A. Jewell

Better Known as Dick Jewell
Let me hear at once from you

Randolph-Macon Academy
Front Royal, Va.   Sept. 17, 1934.

Mr. J.R. Lassiter
Luray, Va.
Dear Mr. Lassiter:

Mr. Wm. E. Carson, Riverton, Va., has advised Mr. H.E. Merchant, Front Royal, Va., that he should appeal to you for permission (if any is to be granted) to haul the fence rails from the inner lines on the Winfield Fox Farm, located on Buck's Mt. (Blue Ridge range), south of Front Royal. H.E. Merchant is living on the property adjoining (on

the north side) the W. Fox farm. Merchant appealed to some other gen-
tleman in Luray, who referred him to Mr. Carson, who now refers him
to you.

Thanking you in advance, for the courtesy of a reply, in the enclosed
envelope, I am

Yours very truly,

Chas. L. Melton[1]

Box 641

Front Royal, Va.

1. Warren County resident Charles L. Melton owned ninety acres on tract 109
and was paid $3,920 by the state. He was the principal of Randolph Macon Academy,
and Merchant, to whom he refers in his letter, was a landowner himself in Warren
County. See also the letter of December 7, 1937.

ARCHDEACONRY OF THE BLUE RIDGE

Diocese of Virginia   Charlottesville, Va., November 19, 1934

Mr. Ferdinand Zerkel,

Luray, Va.

My dear Mr. Zirkel:

I am writing to ask permission to have some dead and down wood
around the mission and adjoining place at Simmon's Gap, cut for fuel for
the mission workers. I warned the men not to touch anything but dead
wood, which I feel sure you would be glad to have removed.

Secondly, I want to consult you about the situation at Simmon's Gap.
I was there yesterday, and the people seem much upset. Many of them
have been unable to shuck their corn because of the dry weather and it
would be very difficult to haul the feed out from where they live, so I am
asking you please to give permission or get it for them to let them stay till
sometime in the late winter or early spring provided that they cut no living trees and do no damage to land or building; and provided further they
sign an agreement to get out not later than April 1st. I can give guarantee
that they will get out and I will make them sign such an agreement, but it
would work a real hardship if they had to get out now. I talked with a
number of them and I am afraid they are very few at Simmon's Gap who

Teeny Florence Corbin
Nicholson, Madison County
resident, wife of George Bailey
Nicholson (John T. Nicholson's
uncle). (Courtesy of Shenandoah National Park Archives;
used by permission of
Nicholson's family)

will sign up for the homestead. I am sure that this plan which I suggest
will be the wisest and best way to get them out. Please let me hear at your
earliest convenience.

> With all best wishes, I am,
> Sincerely yours,
> W.R. MASON.[1]

1. Wiley R. Mason, archdeacon of the mission with offices in Tanner's Ridge
in Shenandoah National Park, was one of several missionaries who worked in the
area and advocated for park residents. See also the letters of March 19 and December 5, 1935.

Skyland, Va. Dec 29th 1934

Mr Fordenand Zerkel,

Luray, Park Office,

My dear sir, This is to notify you that last night some one came to my place and robed two windows and some roofing paper off the school bldg. I have property and feed for my cows in the school bldg. And it was used for school and church, I thought it best to notify you that this happned. I live in the park and have an use permit till the homesteads are ready, I think it is bad enough to break up and steall from any body much less a poor widow woman,

Sincerly Yours,

Mrs. Tenny F. Nicholson[1]

1. This is a typed copy, and any errors may have been made by the typist. In Nicholson's handwritten letters, her name is spelled "Teeny." Teeny Florence Corbin was George Bailey Nicholson's wife and Richard Nicholson's mother. G. Bailey Nicholson owned twenty-five acres on tract 33 in Madison County and was paid $910 by the state. "Tiny" Nicholson owned fourteen acres on tract 96 and was paid $600. See also the letters of March 8 and 26, April 13, and August 7, 1938, and Richard's letters of November 11, 1935; August 10, 1936; and August 7, 1945 (the last in the epilogue, on pp. 159–60).

Requesting Buildings, Harvesting Crops, and Extending Permits

During 1935, more and more letters arrived at the SNP headquarters in Luray requesting that residents be able to use building materials from old or vacated homes. In some cases, CCC workers, under the direction of the NPS, dismantled and burned the houses that residents left behind when they moved out of the park. As several residents discuss in their letters, some people would take the materials without asking permission, an act technically illegal because the land and the materials were owned by the state, then the federal government. Therefore, the letters that arrived during this time asked permission, rationalizing residents' need and use for the materials and presenting the logic for letting them have the materials rather than letting them go to waste by having the CCC destroy them.

Similarly, as residents left behind their homes, they also left behind various crops planted the year before. Therefore, several letters arrived requesting that the letter writer be allowed to harvest those crops, since they were planted before the residents vacated their property. Further, requests came to SNP asking that land be cultivated, in some cases by the previous owners and in some cases by neighbors or people living near park boundaries.

In order for residents to live on the park land until their homesteads were available, they were required to sign up for a special use permit (SUP, see page 11), a document granting them the status to live on federal property for one year. Because of delays in building the homesteads and in determining residents' eligibility for government-assisted loans, many residents stayed in the park but had to write for extensions of their SUPs.

While they were living under the auspices of multiple government agencies, including the Park Service and the Department of Welfare, they had to interact with these officials in order to continue their daily activities such as farming, gardening, and maintaining fencing for their livestock.

The letters written during this year also reflect a growing sense of frustration among the residents as they disputed with their neighbors or defended themselves against the assumptions made about them by officials in the government. James Buracher's February 27 letter and Mrs. Frank Comer's December 24 letter demonstrate the ways that residents point out SNP's responsibility in resolving disputes and clarifying rules. Not only do residents seek assistance from park officials, but they also begin to demand that park officials take responsibility for the resulting situations among neighbors and with the use of the land. As residents requested permission to remove building materials, cultivate land, and move to vacated homes, the previous owners became, understandably, upset by others' gaining from their loss. In addition to this growing number of neighborly disputes, residents began to assert their concern that the Park Service live up to its responsibility in taking care of certain matters for residents. Generally, underlying tensions can be seen in these letters, and those tensions escalated in the years that followed.

Jan 8 1935

Dear Mr Lassister

I will write you about a house the house that I live in it ant good anough for a dog to stay in Mr Roberd Dodson are going to move, I wont to move in his house when he moves. I am waiting for a homestead and Mr Robert Dodson didnot sign for any. let me know if I can move. you write Mr Robert Dodson and tell him not to take any doors ar windows from the house it is a good house and a good cow pasture too. I am waiting for a home stead. answer at once

Lots of Love.
Sincerely
From Eddie H Nicholson[1]

1. Eddie Nicholson, Teeny Nicholson's nephew (by marriage), owned forty-four acres in Madison County on tracts 47 and 327 and was paid $932 by the state.

~~~

Jan 14 1935

Mr. Zerkel   dear Sir Can I move in Gorge Herren house the house I
live in ant mutch good the window is out and doors of I can get Eny from
another house will it be all right wiht youyou let me know at once what
I can move or not

<div align="right">

Your truly mr
Boss Morris[1]
Swift Run Va
</div>

1. Morris refers in this letter to the property of George R. Herring (husband of
Lillie Coleman Herring) on tract 158 in Greene County. See also the letters of February 26 and March 10, 1935, and March 1, 1936.

~~~

Jan 23—35[1]   Stanley Va

Mr. L. F. Zirkle
Dear Sir Just a line in regards to Farming a piece of land the Park taken
of mine the Park taken 6 acres of my land. and it lays Just a long the out
Edge of the Park and I would like to know if the Park People would care if
I farm 3 acres of it in corn as that is the only Place I would have for corn I
dont think it would hurt to farme it as there is no grass on it they Should
let me I Bought one acre I give the Price of one acre years ago when the
Park was first thought of. would appreciate it a lot if you could give me
Permission to farm it or if you cant give me Permission your self would
you find out who could. Thanking you for any information you may give
me. let me hear from you soon in rigards to the above

Respt yours
Vernon B Knight
Stanley Va R2

1. Vernon Bell Knight's letter was written on Continental Life Insurance Company letterhead. Knight owned five acres on tract 367 in Page County and was paid
$180 for it by the state.

Jan 26—1935   Swift Run Va

Dear sir in ans to your letter of recent date, will inform you that I am no near relation to mr Charlie Davis, and also I wanted possession of the house in which he now lives as the place that I now live, will say that it is not very convenionant in which to live, as Mr. Davis is already removed the garden fence, and there is no out building at the place which I live and also I notice in the paper which I am to sign that I would be held responsible for the condition of the buildings, but if not hindred there wont be much left when he gets moved out, as I have been told that he is going to remove all windows and doors, and also remove the granery which is now in good condition, not saying nothing of all the fence, so please let me hear from you again as soon as possible.

Yours Respt
Otis L. Davis[1]

1. Otis Lee Davis was married to Helen Mae Baugher, daughter of Lloyd L. and Rebecca Baugher. See also the letter of February 26, 1936, and the Baughers' letters of May 8, 1935, and February 19 and March 31, 1936.

Feb. 26. 1935

Mr. Zerkel.

Dear Sir in answer to a letter Just received of Feb. 25 in regard to the George. Herring house and to the signing of the Special use permit. I am willing to Sign the extenion use permit at once if it is considered by you all. my reason for not signing the use permit before was that Mr. Smith Morriss land was left out of the park at first but later have been taken.

Yours. Sincerly
Mr. Boss. Morriss.[1]
Swift Run. Va.

1. See also the letters of January 14 and March 10, 1935, and March 1, 1936.

~~~

Front Royal, Virginia   February 26, 1935

National Park Office
Luray, Virginia
Attention: Mr. Lassiter
Dear Mr. Lassiter,

Will you please inform me if this state or the national government is going to let the former orchard owners take care of and harvest the apple crop this year. We own the orchard about three (3) miles east of Browntown in Warren County known as the Wines and Pomeroy Orchard. If the government will let us go ahead with the orchard, we would not want to do any cultivating of any land, simply prune and spray the orchard and remove the crop.

Mr. John Jewell, our former employee, still remains in the house on the farm. Please let us hear from you at your earliest convenience. I am very truly yours.

Wines and Pomeroy
By H.W. Pomeroy[1]

1. Herbert William Pomeroy owned Pomeroy Wine and Orchard on 144 acres on tract 83 in Warren County and was paid $6,344 by the state. See also the letter of March 27, 1936, and John Jewell's letters of August 8, 1935, and March 23, 1936.

~~~

Luray, Virginia.   February 27, 1935.

Dear Sir:

I am writing you all about the Hoake place which you all bought for park purposes in the Shenandoah Park, this place and S. Hite Maddesitt joins, and I am living on Mr. Maddesitt's place and he told me he was going to bring cattle up on his place in a short time and he told me to write you all and get you all to fix your all part of fence. Mr. Hoakes use to fix the fence but now you all have bought the land and now it is in your alls place to fix your part of the fence. It would be four(4) or five (5) days work to fix your alls part of the fence so by causing you all the trouble of hireing someone, I'll fix it for six dollars($6.00) so this work must be done at once so just as soon as I receive the $6.00 I'll fix your all part of the fence and everything will be all right then. This must be done at once please.

Yours truly,
from Mr. James Buracher,[1]
Luray, Virginia.
R.F.D. #2.

1. James R. Buracher owned thirty-one acres on tract 348 in Page County and was paid $503 by the state. See also the letter of January 10, 1938.

~~~

March 10 1935

Mr Zerkel.

Dear Sir   I have moved to the George Herring place. and under the Contract was to use all buildings an be responsible for them.
Mr. Herring have been to the C C. Camp no. 3. trying to get the store room from them. this room would be of use to me as the roof is bad on the corn house. He also has it locked. and orders me not to touch it. Also has a few hundred pounds of hay in the barn. Would like for him to move it out so I will have room for my cows. If you desire me to hold all buildings please let me no at once so I can show the foreman my permit when he comes to tear them down.

<div style="text-align: right">

Yours sincerly
Mr. Boss. Morriss[1]
Swiftrun Va.

</div>

1. See also the letters of January 14 and February 26, 1935, and March 1, 1936.

~~~

Proffit Va   March 17—35

Mr Zerkel.-

Dear Sir+

I'm now answering your letter I recived from you. so called a Copy to Boss Morris.[1]

I'm very mutch suprised to get a thang like that. I have not said or even thraught of tearing dawn eny thang up there. that is some of Boss Morrises lies he reparted to you. his wife told me she had a wretten permett to stay there tell fall and said you had given them the buildings to move a way this fall. and I do know the C C C boys has been giving a way the buildings. an I can prove this to you they gave the George Shifflett house and all to Andry Mawbray. and the also gave G. M. Shifflett buildings to Bernard & Warren Shifflett and the also got N. C. Herrings buildings and the gave Mr C J Begoon buildings to William Sullivan. and Mr Sellars buildings to ame Shifflett. and I wretten to W. C. Hall Chairman Richmond and he said you all had no right to give a way the buildings. and I say if you all were a goning to give them a way wouldent it be more nicer to give it to the one who awned the property and Boss Morris moved from his house he taken the windows & doors I do not know what he did with them. and Bosses wife. told me you had promised Ame Shifflett the store building to move a way. and that is the way you all are doning and sending me your harble letters to which I havent had nothing to do with eny of the buildings up there. I thank you had better send some letters to the ones who are halling out the buildings and the fence. I'm very mutch suprised at you sending to me sutch a thand. I thraught you were a man of a better standing than that. I want you to know that my husband or I nether one have not been messing. with the mess of people up there or the buildings either and Boss Morris Cant come to my face and tell his lies. and that place was mine and not C. R. Herrings. They are up there a beating the park aut of every thang they can and a living on what has moved aut and do you up hold sutch as that. if you do you wont be mutch thraught of as they are. and every body knows what sutch thangs as Boss Morris is. Boos is up there lieing on my husband and he was here down with the grip I'm not lieing on no one. and I'm not telling you one ward mare than I can prave and I am living up to what I say. and I'm a goning to keep your letter and show it to the nicest of people who knows you lisent to Boss Morris lieing on us. and know we had nothing to do with Boss Morris or his bueldings they clam you give to him. I want you to answer this at once

Yours Truly
Lillie Herrg[2]
wife of G. R. H.

1. Boss Morris and the Herrings were neighbors before they were forced to relocate. As their series of letters reveals, they had several disputes among them as building materials were distributed and as families moved from house to house.

2. This letter was typed by Zerkel's office, so some of the misspellings may have been made by the typist. See also the letter of November 26, 1935. Lillie Coleman Herring was the wife of George R. Herring, who owned twenty-six acres on tract 158 in Greene County and was paid $1,800 by the state.

ARCHDEACONRY OF THE BLUE RIDGE
Diocese of Va.   Charlottesville, Va., March 19, 1935

Mr. L. Ferdinand Zerkel,
Luray, Va.
My dear Mr. Zerkel:

I have been hoping to get to see you but things have kept on getting in my way so that I will not postpone writing any longer. I need to find out some things right now. I understand that permission has been given the mountain people to stay on in the Park area for another year. I would like to have this verified so we can plan our work. If they stay on we would like to continue having services.

I also understand that you are giving permission to pull down old buildings to get them out of the way. There is one old frame building at Simmon's Gap which is not much good and if you want me to I would pull it down and use the material in some building I am doing elsewhere. I would like permission to take the wire fence down as I don't feel you have any need for it and I could use it to advantage.

Do you think the Church could be used there indefinitely or should it be taken down? I'm going to build a church this summer and would like to have those windows if that must be taken down. One window is a memorial and of course would like to put it elsewhere.

I am sorry to trouble you about all these small details but I don't want to do anything without permission. There are other matters I want to talk to you about but I will postpone those till I can see you.

With all best wishes, I am,

Sincerely,
W.R. MASON[1]

1. See also the letters of November 19, 1934, and December 5, 1935.

Islandford, Va.   March 28, 1935.

Mr. J.R. Lassiter
Luray, Virginia
Dear Sir,

In regard to the house occupied by William Shifflett located on the
Yost tract of land near Islandford, Va. in the National Park Area, as it is
an old building of very little or no value I would like to know if you would
let one have it, as the Park officials expects to tear it down and burn it I
would be glad to take it away as soon as you give the notice I would appreciate it very much and would like to have a reply as soon as convenient.

Respectfully,
J.W. King[1]

1. Joseph W. King owned seventy acres on tract 249 in Rockingham County, land
that was surveyed but not purchased for the park. King's letter is an example of the
many letters that came from nearby landowners and tenants, even if their land did
not become part of the park. His and other nearby residents' letters illustrate how
the formation of the park affected many people in the community, not just those displaced from their homes.

Syria Va   April 27 1935

I have your letter of April 26[1] I have no place to move and I have Seven
little children and no place to go and the Park caused me Lose my home
I am not going to move in the Road So you do anything you can So there
is no emty houses no where in Madison Co So if you can put my Seven little in Road and my Sick wife in Road come and do So and if there is anything that you can tell me to do I will Be glad to do it I will get out Just as
Soon as I can So please let me here from you and tell what must I do. Kenneth Nicholson

1. Kenneth Nicholson is referring to a letter received from Lassiter requesting
that he "make arrangements to move back outside at once." Several letters written
by residents were prompted by the letters they received from Lassiter, Hoskins, or
Zerkel. The letters from these officials often informed residents of some infraction.
Kenneth W. Nicholson was the son of Barbara and William Aldridge Nicholson of

Madison County. See Barbara Nicholson's letters of 1935 (no date; end of the year); February 5 and 15, 1937; and January 3, 1946 (the last in the epilogue, on p. 160).

<center>~~~</center>

May 8, 1935   Swift Run, Va

Dear Sir,

in regaurd to let you know that Mr. alake Morris and Tomases Mavie and also his sun inlaw that has Been married just about a month. has come over here on this place to tend and they dont pay any attenion to the letter you wrote them nor what I saw so you write me a notis and send me so I can give it to the chief. to serve on them, write no tresspasses on the S.G. Mavis place. I surly do hate to Be bother you writing so much But I just want to tell you How they are doing I went to the magstrist Here at Elkton and he advise us to write to you all and for you all to write me a notis and send me so I could give it to the chief to serve on them your Truly

Lloyd L Baugher[1]

1. The Baughers lived near tract 36 in Rockingham County. See also the letters written by Lloyd's wife, Rebecca Jane Powell Baugher, dated February 19 and March 31, 1936.

<center>~~~</center>

Miss Janet E. Walton[1]   St. Luke's Mission, Tanners' Ridge
Shenandoah National Park   Stanley, Virginia
June 8, 1935.

My dear Mr. Lassiter:

Claude Breeden has asked me to ask you if he could have about an acre of ground about a mile South of Tanners' Ridge, on what formerly belonged to Mr. Brubaker, for potatoes. I am sorry to trouble you again, but he asked you for some ground for rye last fall (at least, I asked him for you) and you said he could not have it, and, of course, he didn't use it, and was very nice about it and said nothing. Almost all these people here, if they can get enough ground for their crops, they will not ask the Government for anything, and also if they can find a market for what they raise, such as potatoes and cabbage. They produce all they need to eat. Claude says this particular piece he would like to have has been under cultivation and has nothing growing on it but mullen, and is not in sight of the Skyline Drive. I hope you can let him have it. Please pardon my writing, but I am so busy, going to clinics and looking after a lot of things, that I really haven't the time to make a special trip to Luray for the above, unless it is necessary.

Thanking you for everything, I am,

Sincerely, Janet E. Walton

He is not asking for the same piece for potatoes that he asked for for rye. I am sorry to trouble you again, I think this is the last time.

1. This letter was written on personalized stationery from the mission. Like Wiley R. Mason, Janet Walton (who later married the Reverend Dennis Whittle) served as a missionary to local families, mostly in Page County. See also the letter of December 4, 1935.

~~~~

Luray, Va   June 18, 1935

Mr JR. Lassiter

Dear Mr Lassiter

Do you care if I get some Barb wire of of the A.W. Long property to put around some corn patches and other stuff where I have got out a growing it is no body using the A.W. Long property science Noah Nicholson and Clearance Corbin been caught for putting out fire they have been telling it around that I have been cleaning up new ground to farm but it is not true. the land I had in year before last was so thin it would not bring nothing hardly. I grubbed of some other patches whear have been farmed about 8 years ago

Please let me hear from you by return mail

From Mr James Luther Corbin[1]

Nethers Va

1. See also the letter of March 3, 1936. James Luther's brother, Dennis Corbin, also wrote letters dated January 31, 1936, and February 9 and March 10, 1937. James Luther and Dennis were the sons of James E. Corbin, who owned eighty-one acres on tract 37 in Madison County and was paid $1,182 by the state. Their brother, Charles "Buck" Corbin, owned fifty-six acres on tract 35 in Madison County and was paid $845 by the state. Buck's wife, Fanney, wrote a letter dated March 3, 1936.

James Luther and Elma
Corbin, Madison
County residents.
(Courtesy of
Shenandoah National
Park Archives; used
by permission of
Corbin's family)

aug 8 1935   Browntown Va

Mr lassitier i am writing to you fear sum emnished [information] i wont
to no if enney law fear Hunting on the Park land i Had Sum fellow taking
in fear Hunting and they want done nothing with them aber thing they
done with them fine them Hunting with out lisons that all they done
about it i would like to look after the maters So would have pertessons
[permission] i thank i am looking after the matters them fellows i Had un

they swore to all kind of lies and i got to go and look un witnes to clare
my Sealf i think i aut have sum thurdy to Pert time to look after the matters fear if i dont get Sum thurdy to look after the matters i dont think it
is nersey to turn enney thing in the Park office at Front Royal that is fear
it go when you turn it in if you want enney Ressitissen [residents] i think
i can find un Sum good resdusans [reasons] fear me it is Hard matter fear
me to look up all them thing fear nothing i would like to Have Sum
thurdy to look up them matters

there is fellow moonshiner on the Park land and cuting timber to so if
dont get sum thurdy i cant do nothing with them i am poor man i cant
Hardly look up this matter fear nothings write Back at once and let me no
your truly from John Jewell[1] Browntown Va

1. Jewell was H. W. Pomeroy's employee and lived on his property in Warren
County, tract 83. See also the letter of March 23, 1936, and Pomeroy's letters of February 26, 1935, and March 27, 1936.

~~~~

Fletcher, Va.   Sept. 7, 1935

My dear Mr. Zerkel,

I am very anxious to know if I may stay on my farm for another year.
I want to sow grain this fall if I may stay on to harvest it, and I also wish
to know if I may have the privilege of having the boxwood on this farm
trimmed and sell the trimmings.[1]

Mr. William E. Carson of Riverton, Va. came to see me a few days ago
and told me that I might stay on as long as I like, and that he was going to
have the boxwood taken up and taken away.

Please answer this at once.

Yours Truly
Mrs. Ardista Lamb[2]

1. At the time, selling boxwood trimmings was a way to earn money. Trimmings
were often sold for decoration or so that they could "take root," that is, so that new
boxwood bushes could be grown from the cuttings.

2. At the end of this typed letter are the words "By C. F. T.," which are the initials
of Zerkel's secretary. See also the letters written by Ardista's son, James Lamb, dated
March 7 and April 27, 1936. James Lamb owned twenty-eight acres on tract 10 in
Greene County and was paid $490 by the state.

Sept 11—1935   Nethers, Va.

Mr. J.R. Lassiter,
Luray, Va.
My dear sir:

Please pardon me for leaving the Office the Other day without thinking you for your attention, or biding you good day. The reason I did it, I
was figuring on coming back in to see you again before I left town. I was
not displeased in any way, but saw that you were very busey.

I am coming back next Monday to see you if I do not see you before.

If you come over here your nearest and best way is over the Skyline
Drive, then you want have but about three miles to walk—that is both
ways. If you come by Nethers, Va. you will have to walk from the Hughes
River Baptist Church up the hollow to where we live, which is about two
and a half miles. O course you might get a horse of some one who lives
close the church. Hope you will come and see the condition for your self.
Say Mr. Lassiter, I need the house Albert moved out off to repair mine,
and hope it will please your honor to let me have it, as it belonged to me
any way before the park taken it. Do not you honestly belive that I should
have the preface of that house before any body else. I say this, because I
heard that Sammie Printz was coming over to see you about this same
house. I will see you monday if not before.

Affectionately yours.

John T. Nicholson,

c/o Russ Nicholson,[1]

1. Russ Nicholson is John Russell Nicholson, John Taylor Nicholson's father, who
was granted life tenure. Russ Nicholson owned 130 acres on tract 31 in Madison
County and was paid $1,638 by the state. See also John T. Nicholson's other letters
of January 28 and September 20, 1937, and the letters written by his mother, Elizabeth Corbin Nicholson, dated March 5 and May 7, 1936.

Oldrag Va   Sept. 25. 1935

Dear Sir

I will ask you a favor Will you Please give me a Permit to Some of the
fruit on my old Place in the Park where I used to live on my son in law

John T. Nicholson, Madison County resident and son of John Russ Nicholson, seen here with baskets he sold to help make his living. (Library of Congress, Prints & Photographs Division, FSA-OWI Collection, reproduction number LC-USF33-003613-M1; photograph by C. Arthur Rothstein, 1935; used by permission of the Nicholson family and Grace Rothstein)

lives on the Place now, I told him he could stay there and take care of the fruit, There is two or Three hundred bushels of apples Will you please give me a Permit so that I can get enough for family use and you will greatly favor me, as there is not much fruit where I live now now I will close for this time with many thanks,

Yours truly
Mrs Elizabeth Seal,[1]

P.S. Please let me Know at once as the apples falling off.

1. Elizabeth Seal was married to Charles E. Seal, who owned ninety-one acres on tract 86 in Madison County, fifty-five of which were purchased by the state for $984.

Grottoes Virginia   Route 1   Oct. 7—35

Mr. J.R. Lassiter—

Dear Sir—

I am writting to you to see if there is any way I could get a couple old buildings up at Black Rock Springs? There is no windows or doors in them.

I wrote to Mr Menefee and he suggested the I write you and said you could advise me about them.

Thanking you for information.

Yours Truly
G.A. Sandy
Grottoes, Va.
Route 1

P.S. These couple old buildings are in the Shenandoah National Park.

Skyland, Va   Oct 12 1935

Mr J.R. Lasster

Dear Sir this louis Nicholison House I wrote you about is in Berry Hollow above Syria Va this House is Rite where Seder Run and White oat creek comes toghter at the foot of the mountian it is J.O. Nicholison Place it is Rite on the Park line in Madison Co Please let me hear you at once as Some one aut of the Park is going to move thire if you Dont Stop thim

Hope you will give me a Permit to move until the home Stids is Ready I will take good care of the Place for you

yours very truly
Bernie Taylor[1]
Skyland Va

1. Bernie Lee Taylor, Walter Delan Taylor's son, owned sixty acres in Madison County and was paid $234 by the state. Lassiter wrote to Bernie Taylor on October 9, 1935, and said "if you will write me giving the exact location of his house, I will be able to advise you if it will be all right for you to move." See also the letter of January 11, 1936, and W. D. Taylor's letters of December 21, 1935; February 19 and March 16, 1936; October 7 and 24, 1937; and January 24, 1938.

~~~

Skyland, Va   Nove 11, 1935

Mr J.R. Lassiter

Luray, Va

My Dear Sir, I am writing you to see if you will give me permission to cut some dry wood and sell it by the cord There is some parties living out side the park that wants me to cut them some wood for 2^{00} per cord. I thought that I would ask you as leaf is light. Mr Lassiter I would be very glad and thankful to you if you would let me cut the wood. As I dont have any employment of no kind. I am son of Mrs Teeney Nicholson I live 3 miles east of Skyland. Of course if it is against the rules I would not want to cut it. My father is dead and I am the only one to look after my mother. Please do what you can for me as I am in tough luck for the winter.

My mother and I thank you for leting us stay and we want to obey park Rules.

Ancer soon.

Sincerly Yours.

Richard Nicholson[1]

1. See also the letters of August 10, 1936, and August 7, 1945 (the latter in the epilogue, on pp. 159–60), and the letters written by Richard's mother, Teeny Florence Corbin Nicholson, dated December 29, 1934; March 13, 1937; and March 8 and 26, April 13, and August 7, 1938. Richard's mother, Teeny, owned tract 96, and his father, George Bailey, owned tract 33 in Madison County.

~~~

Browntown Va   Nov 21, 1935

Mr Zirkle,

Dear Sir,

I am writing to you, in regards to wood in the park area. Will you please let me get 2 loads of down wood, I waunt dry Chestnut that is on the ground please let me know by return mail.

Yours Respectfully

C.M. Good[1]

Browntown Va

1. Charles Malone Good lived in Page County and was a nearby resident of the park. Like several others, Good wrote to request collecting "down" wood, that is, wood that was dead, in order to follow park procedure. Collecting wood for home heat was common among neighbors before the park was established, but with the formalizing of the park's boundaries, residents were required to write to ask permission. Most often their requests were denied.

Freeunion Va   Nov 26—35

Mr L. F. Zerkel
  Dear Sir
I heard all of the people in the park have got to move oul. and I'm asking you to do me a favor. When Boss Norris Moves out of the house I used to own. Will you please give it to me. My Husband George R. Herring is dead and left me Six children and no home. and I could get the house out of the Park and it would be some help to the children. you all gave the mission people severl buildings and they have moved them out so I would be awfull thankfull if you would help me some. So let me Hear from you at once thank you.

Yours Truly
Lillie Herring[1]
Free union Va.

1. See also the letter of March 17, 1935.

Mission Home Va.   Nov. 29, 1935

Dear sir
I will drop you a few lines do you thank that Charlie mugoon had a write to paster cattle on the park land he paster 25 head as we no ever. the over summer the plase that yowl pay for on Summion Gap. I dont thank that he had no write. i dont no of no body els did but him. I believe that he out to be pay for paster. answer soon and let me no what you thank about it.

from Herbert Shifflett[1]
To mr. Zerkel.

1. William Herbert Shifflett owned seven acres on tract 303 in Greene County and was paid $50 by the state.

~~~~

Sperryville, Virginia.[1]   November 30th, 1935.

Hon. Wilbur C. Hall, Chairman,
State Commission on Conservation and Development,
Richmond, Virginia.
Dear Mr. Hall:—

I acknowledge receipt of your letter of November 21st, giving notice to vacate the property in the Shenandoah National Park area as agreed. It is my purpose to comply with your request.

I am writing to ask if it will be permissible for me to remove from the property the following small buildings.

3- hen houses, 8 × 10

1- Hog Pen.

These buildings will be of much use to me in my new location and are valuless to the State. In all probability they will be destroyed in clearing up the site and will not be of any benefit to anyone.

I trust you may be able to grant my request.

Yours very truly,
James W. Ramey [signed]
James W. Ramey

1. This letter is typed, with James W. Ramey's signature at the bottom. In the SNP archives, there is one letter handwritten and signed "Jas. W. Ramey" and a second letter handwritten and signed "Lucile Ramey" (his daughter). In both hand-penciled letters, the handwriting appears the same. In addition, the signature of the typewritten letter and the signature of the handwritten letter are different. It is possible, therefore, that both handwritten letters were completed by Lucile Ramey. Given the formal language in the typed letter, it is possible that Mr. Ramey had someone type this letter for him, as several residents did within the park as they sought advice on how to have their requests granted. As was standard, this letter was forwarded from the SCCD to Lassiter so that he could attend to the request. James W. Ramey owned 219 acres on tracts 153 and 167 in Rappahannock County and was paid $10,609 by the state. See also the letter of May 1936.

~~~

Miss Janet E. Walton,[1]   St. Luke's Mission, Tanners' Ridge,
Shenandoah National Park,   Stanley, Virginia.
Dec. 4, 1935.

My dear Mr. Hall:

Fred Meadows is living in the house belonging to Bob Meadows
outside of the Park area. Bob Meadows is Fred Meadows uncle. Bob
Meadows is living in the park area and has to move. And since he has to
move from the park area he expects to come to the place on which Fred
Meadows is now living, and which he owns. This puts Fred out and he
has no place to go. Fred Meadows is a very fine man. He lives a short distance from me and brings my water each day, as I have no water on the
place, and looks after the wood and things generally around the mission.
All of his wife's people live here. I run a clothing bureau, second hand and
new clothing, and the amount I pay Fred each week for bringing water
etc. almost clothes his family. His children (two large enough to be away
from home, that is to go to things, 10 and 8 years of age) and we have
something for them every day in the work that is educative and uplifting.
If he had to move away from here the kind of community he would go to,
be able to go to, would be quite different in the way of uplift and better-
ment thatn the surroundings he now has, and the influences he and his
family are daily in contact with.

There is a family living about a mile from Fred's place, the place he
now lives, in fact there are two families, who have to move because they
are in the Park area, and one of those families, Walker Jenkins has to move
at once. If Fred could get the house Walker Jenkins is now living in in the
park, and about a mile from where he now lives (Fred) he could put him
up a house on his father-in-law's land and stay in this community and I
am writing to you to ask if you will not givehim permission after Walker
Jenkins has left, to go there and tear down the buildings and put himself
up a little house on his father-in-law's land with the lumber he gets from
the Walker Jenkins' place within the park area. I assure you Fred is a good
worker and he will leave the place in an orderly and clean condition and
take all rubbish and trash away. I also assure you that we will say nothing
about anything. We have been told that Fred could probably just go there
after Walker has left and get the lumber, but we do not want to encourage

our mission people in doing things in that manner. We are living near the park and we want to encourage them to live up to the law and give the park authorities no trouble of any nature whatsoever. And you realize that often if a person is given an inch they will take an L. Fred is a hard working man and makes his living for himself and his wife and four children, ages 10, 8, 2 and 3 weeks, like all the other mountain people. With the mission to help them they do very well and are happy and self-supporting. He has never received one thing from FERA. I don't know what I would do and the Mission without Fred to help keep us going and there is no other place in this community he could get—nothing vacant.

I do hope that you will let us have it, Fred Meadows, the house Walker Jenkins is living in to tear down and move, and from which he will move very soon. We will be glad to cooperate in any way possible you wish us to that we are able to do. I am sure you and the park authorities will never regt it. I don't think the granting of this request would cause any trouble of any kind in this community. Walker Jenkins is going to have to move very soon, probably tomorrow as the Sheriff has given him notice to get away by that time. We are afraid if Fred is not there to begin taking the place down immediately when Walker Jenkins vacates some one else will do it and Fred will lose it, because some people, out of our community, take what they want and don't ask for it, so I hope you will give me a prompt reply as possible and if you would call me over the phone I would be glad to pay the message. I am sending this letter Special Delivery.

I do hope you can let us have it, and please do the best for us you can.

Very truly yours,
Janet E. Walton

Fred Meadows wants to put his house on his father-in-law's land, <u>outside the park area</u>, of course. I have taken this matter up with two or three people and they are in sympathy with the situation and have no objection to Fred having the Walker Jenkins' house to tear down and move to build one for himself, but they haven't theauthority to give Fred the permission.

1. See also the letter of June 8, 1935.

⌒⌒

ARCHDEACONRY OF THE BLUE RIDGE
Diocese of Virginia
Charlottesville, Va. Dec. 5, 1935.

Mr. Ferdinand Zirkel
Luray, Va.
My dear Mr. Zirkel:-

I have not herad from you as to when you wish us to vacate the house at Simmons Gap. We would be glad to stay through the winter as there are enough people in the neighborhood to whom to minister, but we will move out any time you wish. I would like to have some notice however as we have a good bit of stuff to move.

Sincerely yours
WRMason[1]

1. Wiley R. Mason. See also the letters of November 19, 1934, and March 19, 1935.

⌒⌒

Swift Run, Va.[1]   December 5, 1935

Mr. W. C. Hall
Chairman of the State Conversation and Development Commission
Richmond, Virginia
Dear Mr. Hall:

Mr. Hansbrough and I are moving. I have got me a place but I am asking you could I have some of these old buildings and also Mr. Hansbrough wants some to for to build some thing for our fowls and stock. The land owners in the park has been asking for the old buildings and they gave them to them if they wanted them. And also some of this old wire to fence up a place to hold my stock. Which is the place I am going to has not got no fence and has no buildings for fowls and to store away my crops. If you are not the right man please send it on to the right one. I would more than appreciate your kindness hope to hear from you soon.

Very truly yours,
Ambrose W. Shiflett[2]

1. This letter is typed on SCCD stationery. Often the letters sent to the SCCD and then forwarded to SNP were typed as a copy of the original.

2. Ambrose Shifflett owned 325 acres on tract 178 in Rockingham County and was paid $7,166 by the state. See also the letter of December 11, 1935.

~~~

[received Dec 9 1935]

Dear Mr. Lassiter.
I am riting to ask you if you can Send me Homestead Papers as I Havent any place to move. i have a Family of Little Children and no place to go i sined up For the home Sted papers once will you Let me have them now will you send them to me i just ant able to get out just now So please Let me no at once iF i can get the home Sted Papers

From Pete Nicholson[1]
Oldrag, Va.

1. Pete L. Nicholson, George Bailey Nicholson's brother, owned five acres on tract 41 in Madison County and was paid $550 by the state.

~~~

Nortensville Va.   December 11, 1935.

J.R. Lassiter,
Luray Virginia,
Dear Mr Lassiter,

I am enclosing to you Mr Hall letter which I ask him for some of the old buildings and some wire to fence to keep my stock in where I moved to and he refered me to write to you. Where we have moved to we have no place for our fowls and cows. I would be awful thankful if you would help me out in the wire and lumber which the buildings is not much good. please let me hear from you on return mail.

Very Truly yours.
Ambrose W. Shifflett[1]

1. See also the letter of December 5, 1935.

Elkton, Va   Dec 12—1935

Mr Lasider
Dear Sir:
   One Luther Dean who had a farm on the mountain and sold it to be
used in the Park. This place has a old house on it and he like to know if
you could give him permition to moove the house as he would like to have
it to build some kind of ashed on the place he lives and he has ask me to
write you. and I will thank you for the information.
                                          Respt J.R. Early Mayor[1]

   1. J. R. Early was the mayor of Elkton, Virginia, in Rockingham County and wrote
for Luther Dean, a resident of the park. Early, like Walton and Mason and other
prominent community members, wrote as an advocate for Dean, assisting him with
his request. Lassiter's return letter, though more conciliatory than other letters to
residents, stated, "In reply I wish to advise that we are not permitted to dispose of
any of the physical improvements on any of the land condemned for the Park and
accordingly I must deny your request."

Dec 13 1935   Stanley, Va R1

Dear Mr lasset
I am going to make you a fair offer if you all will give me Back $400 witch
I have spent on this place, it was my own money that I payed out and if
you all will give me my money Back I will get out and Sind all agree-
meent[1] in the next few Day if you all will pay me what I have ask you for
I have spent all the money I have ever made hear on this place and I never
got one Cent out of it and if you will Do this and Don't want no one Else
to know it I will never say enything a Bout it to no one. I have Been told
By a lawer that I Could get my money By going to law with it But I Don't
want no trouble with no Bidy I have a Squater Right hear for 48 years and
also I have my Father possession witch he give me a Bout 25 years ago
and you pleas show this to all the head athoriets
                                                  your truley
                                          Walker F. Jenkins
                                          Stanley, Virginia
                                          Route 1

pleas let me hear from you in the next few day

1. Jenkins is referring to the paperwork condemning his land, which he has been asked to sign by the government. Jenkins's wife, Leslie Cave Jenkins, was Walter Lee Cave's sister. See W. L. Cave's letter of March 24, 1937.

~~~

Swift Run, Va.   Dec. 14th, 1935

Mr. Hall.

Dear Sir:

You will please pardon the liberty I take in writing you.

Since the time is near at hand for the business places in the park area to be closed, I am asking for an extension of time of at least a while longer, or until the license expires the 31st of this month.

I understand a few people will be allowed to stay, so you see a little store here would mean convenience for them.

If in any way you can permit me to occupy this place for any period of time, I'll appreciate same.

May I hear from you?

Respectfully

E. C. Haney

(per Lula A. Haney)[1]

1. Lula Haney wrote this letter for her son, Elbert C. Haney. Lula's husband, John K. Haney, owned forty-one acres on tract 83 in Greene County and seventy-four acres on tract 76 in Rockingham County and was paid $1,760 and $5,065, respectively (according to Lambert's *Undying Past of Shenandoah National Park*). See also the letter of January 13, 1936.

~~~

Dec. 16 1935

Dear Sir

Mr Zerkel

Luray Va

We receved your letter and Was glad to here from you and no about these things I heat to bother you so much but I dont want to do any thing with out noing What I amd doing and I want to no if I can cut sum dead

Lockus wood and if we can farm any here this coming year and pleas let me no about these things as soon as you can

Yours very truly
Robert Matthews[1]
Bentonville Va

1. Matthews lived in Warren County. See also the letters of February 24, 1936, and January 1, March 29, and May 26, 1937, and the letter written by Mrs. Robert Matthews dated September 6, 1936.

Shenandoah Va.   Dec 16th 1935

Mr. J. R. Lassiter.

Dear Sir. I am writeing to ask you if you sold Reuben S. Lucas fire wood off of the Madeira Hill and Co. 1088 Acres that the park took over near Ingham Station. Six miles north of Shenandoah. Mr. J. A. Hilliard's was over seerer of it before the park tooks it over. He said that he told Reuben Lucas that he did not have any thing to do with it now. that it blonged to the park. Reuben Lucas baught wood of me last winter and did not pay for it. He has treated me dirty and cut timber large enough for saw timber. My land joins this land and I am afraid he will cut over on me. And if he does I can't do nothing as he does not own any property or real estate. Will you try and get the Park people to take over my tract that joins the Kelsey Line no 504—65 Acres Price $4960. Since the death of my husband it would help me so much. Lucas has been hauling wood for over a month. If the park wants some one to over see the Co. land I will keep people from cutting the timber if they will appoint me. I've told you the truth and every one is best off not to have any dealing's with Lucas. He cut a couple acres over on us when my husband was liveing. When J.A. Hilliards let him cut some wooud on the Co. land and he crossed over on us. Please stop him getting wood he passes my place every monday and tuesday. He has hauled one load to day and the empty wagon has gone back for more. Sincerely yours,

Mrs. Frank P. Comer[1]

1. Fannie Baugher Comer. Comer owned eighteen and a half acres on tract 504 in Page County, land that was surveyed but not purchased by the state. See also the letter of December 24, 1935.

Walter Delan Taylor, Madison
County landowner and father
of Bernie Lee Taylor. Taylor
owned sixty-two acres in
Madison County and was paid
$810 for his property by the
state. Taylor wrote a total of
six letters in 1935, 1936, 1937,
and 1938, more than any other
resident besides "Gird" Cave
and Lilly Pearl Nicholson
Campbell. (Courtesy of
Shenandoah National Park;
used by permission of
Rodney D. Taylor)

december 21 1935

dear Mr Lasiter
i want to ask if i get out a lot of this dead wood up here near my house and
a long this road will it Be all rite with you as it will Be got out and Burnt
up and waisted and if it Be all write for me to get it out i will take good
care of all they green forest while geting it out and By getting this out
from among they forest it will Be agrate advantage to they forest if a for-

est fire should take place and i want to ask if you will give me some kind
of work to do in they Park as i need work i hope you will Please let me no
about the wood and also about work i hope you and family are all well
yours verry truly

WD Taylor[1]

skyland Va

1. Walter Delan Taylor, Bernie Lee Taylor's father. Taylor's letter is written on
Skyland letterhead, with G. Freeman Pollock's name on it. All the Skyland informa-
tion and Pollock's name are scratched through, with a handwritten note that says,
"Please excuse this paper." See also the letters of February 19 and March 16, 1936;
October 7 and 24, 1937; and January 24, 1938; and Bernie Lee Taylor's letters of
October 12, 1935, and January 11, 1936.

Shenandoah Va   Dec 24—1935

Mr. J. R. Lassiter

   Dear Sir, What I told you about Reuben Lucas getting wood was the
honest truth. But I did not Know that you was going to tell him. He came
to my place last evening with a big rock in his hand expecting to knock
me in the head with it. I did not go out and he threw it against the hen
house is he left. He know's I have no men folk to protect me. He is two
big a coward to go where there is men folk. I did not want him to cut over
on me is why I written. But I did not know that my name would be mentioned to him. I am all alone except my little girls. And he is sorry enough
to do something to my property. yours truly, Mrs Frank Comer[1]

1. Fannie Baugher Comer. See also the letter of December 16, 1935. Comer's letter
reflects concerns similar to those of some other women living alone and caring for children in the park area. With the shift of authority from the state to the National Park
Service, Lassiter received several letters from residents insisting on protection.

[no date but probably 1935 or 1936]

Dear Mr Hoskins.
Odie Corbin wants to know if you will build him a house on his land down
in Culpeper just like you are buck corbins. if I get me a acor of land of odie

will you build me a house on it. we would like to know right at once if you will build our houses.

From Charles Nicholson.[1]

1. Charles Nicholson owned one acre on tract 237 in Madison County and was paid $60 by the state.

～～

[no date but probably 1935 or 1936]

Dear Mr Hoskins Just a Few Lines to let you now i have got my Cow at home and i have Such a OFel time keeping her at home Will you please get me a Little Wire to make a Fence Just as Soon as you Can i ant able to bie the ware So please bring me Some wire just as Soon as you Can So please bring it just as Soon as you can Mrs. W A Nicholson[1] Syria Va

1. Barbara Allen Smith Nicholson, wife of William Aldridge Nicholson. See also the letter of her son, Kenneth W. Nicholson, dated April 27, 1935.

Resolving Disputes and Demanding Park Officials' Responsibility

During 1936, the number of letters received at the park nearly doubled from those received in 1935. As the Commonwealth of Virginia officially turned over the land to the National Park Service and park officials became the legal administrators of the land, letters arrived with greater frequency from the people who remained there until homesteads were ready. As in 1935, letters arriving during 1936 contained requests for building materials, harvesting crops, and extending special use permits. Yet as residents continued to live on the federal property for several years, various tensions mounted with the government and, in some cases, among neighbors, reflecting the general anxiety surrounding the entire removal process.

The letters here represent the residents' negotiations with park officials as they attempted to settle various disputes. Some disputes between neighbors resulted from the inconsistencies in policies. Early on in the removal process, Lassiter and the SCCD did allow people to cultivate land and to remove building materials. However, Lassiter had not anticipated that residents would be living on park property for extended periods. Granting requests to some and not to others inevitably caused problems among some of the residents. Therefore, in a letter to a local missionary on June 12, 1935, Lassiter wrote, "We did do this [grant cultivation requests] in several instances which resulted in so many disputes among the mountain people that it has become necessary to refuse all requests to cultivate other lands." Lassiter was bound by federal government rules, but he was also firm in his belief that granting requests to some residents and not to others would be unfair. Because of the earlier shift in policy making, some residents assumed Lassiter and other park officials granted requests based on favoritism. Therefore, some of the letters reflect residents' attempt to persuade Lassiter to grant their requests based on their cooperativeness and adherence to the park's rules.

Other disputes resulted from residents moving into vacated homes. As some moved off the mountains to homesteads or alternative housing, the others who remained sometimes requested to move into the vacated homes because of their condition or their location. Consequently, when the previous owners heard about these requests, several arguments over materials and land use resulted. As residents sought resolution, they implored park officials to live up to their responsibility and to take action on their behalf because the park administration was now the official authority over the land.

〰〰

Skyland Va   Jan 11/36

Mr JR Lassiter
Dear Sir I am Ready to move out of the Park Soon as my home is Ready would like to move Soon as I can as I want to get out So I can get some work to Do as thire aint any work up hear that I can get I would like to move By the last of next month & Dident get to move in the louis Nicholson House as he Dident move So I couldent move thire & Still live on the White oak Road near the Skyline Drive if I got to move this SPring I want to go now I want to get out of the Park So I can farm Something this year and April is two late to move and fix for to farm a crop Please let me no about moving By my father W.D. Taylor
Your very truly

Bernie Taylor[1]

1. See also the letter of October 12, 1935.

Swift Run, Va.   Jan 13th, 1936.

F. D. Roosevelt,

Pres. U. S. A.

Your honor:

Please pardon for trespassing on your precious time. I would ask not for sympathy nor favors, but this—an extension of time for my son, C. E. Haney who "signed" for the houses in which we are now living in the park area.

He also signed for a "homestead" which I understand are being made ready for those who are to have them.

Now it is rumored this house must be torn down in a short time, if so, where will he go?

He has a wife and a little daughter to take care of.

Perhaps you'd like to know the location of this place. I'll tell you—We had a 100 acres here on top of the "Blue Ridge" now the entrance of the "Park" on Swift Run Gap. I am not ashamed of the old house, tho it does look kinda weather beaten.

I always loved my "mountain home" and never wanted to sell it, but as you know how it all happened, guess it is "gone" now.

Now if you can in some way allow "Bud"(we call him) to occupy the above-named place for at least a month or two yet, in the meantime, we could perhaps make some arrangements.

I'll tell you what I've been thinking—if we can borrow money to buy a few acres for "him", and "they" would let us have the buildings to move from here (this place) we could arrange things. May we have them? Please.

I know there is some other "authority" perhaps I should have asked, but I did not know to whom to go, so in humble simplicity I come to you for directions and information. May I hear from you at an early date?

May God bless and keep you as one who leads our "nation."

Fraternally yours

Lula A. Haney[1]

1. See also the letter of December 14, 1935.

~~~

January 28, 1936   Harriston, Va

Dear Sir

Will you rent me the place till Nov. 1, 1936 The Via place[1] 152 acre. You let me no by the 10 of March 1936. and will you give me a permit to move any of the old building on the Via track it is five building on the Via track. and you let me no about the renting and the building.

From James H. Blackwell

Harriston Va

1. Blackwell is referring to the land of Robert H. Via, who owned 152 acres on tract 41 in Albemarle County and was paid $1,383 by the state. Robert Via brought suit against the Commonwealth of Virginia, saying that the state infringed on his constitutional rights by forcing him to sell his land for the park. The U.S. Supreme Court refused to hear his case, essentially upholding Virginia's Public Park Condemnation Act of 1928. That law allowed Virginia to condemn private property owners' land through eminent domain. In Lassiter's response letter of February 3, 1936, he said, "As for the buildings on the land, I cannot give any one any permission to remove any buildings from the Park Area."

~~~

January 31 1936   Nethers Va

Dear Mr J R lassiter

i want to no frome you if i can farme this lan under my pearmit like i Did last yeare and to trim the apple trees and to have the apples frome this orichard this year

ancer Soon

frome Dennis Corbin[1]

Nethers Va

1. Dennis Corbin was the brother of James Luther Corbin and Charles "Buck" Corbin. Their father was James E. Corbin, who owned eighty-one acres on tract 37 in Madison County and was paid $1,182 by the state. See also the letters of February 9 and March 10, 1937, and James Luther Corbin's letters of June 18, 1935, and March 3, 1936.

feb 1__19__36   Moormans River Va

My dear friend
    i am droping you a few lines Just to ask a little faver of you and a little
of your time and tenchen there is a old log house on the park property and
a verry smoul house Right above that one i would like to Bie if you will
sell them Right i have riten to Mr. Wilbur C. Hall Chairman about them
and he told me to Rite to you about them and he was shore you could give
me the necessary information of them and the price the old log house is
on Mr. MaJer C.S. Roller Jr. Mr. t.J. Roller land in alimora [Albemarle]
Co. and the place i think has about 16.00 Eakers in it the house has 3 little
rooms in it the house is a verry old house and are not verry much good
Just old log house But i could use some of it and the other house is about a
mild above that one it is on Mr frank Pattesen land it has 4 Smoul Rooms
to it and the old Ruff is not anney good and the flowers are Just about gon
so much Rain and weat on it i think that track of land that this one is on is
about 400 Eakers of land i have given you as near as i can the Reformary
and condeashin of them the other man told me all the old Bildens that
wouson verry much good would Be Sold But no good ones that could Be
used woulden Be sold at all so i would like to Bie them from you and hope
this will Be the last letter i will hafto Rite as this makes 4 letters i have
Rote would like to Bie them and moove them Right away so i will close for
this time yours verry truly

                                        Mrs Polly Bowen[1]
                                        Moormans River Va

    1. Polly Bowen (Cora Alice Grim Bowen) refers to the Roller tract 128 and the
Patterson tract 33, both in Albemarle County. Although Mrs. Bowen refers to having written four letters, only one is contained in the archives. Ed Bowen, Polly's
brother-in-law, also wrote on July 27 and November 20, 1936. In his July 27 letter,
he states that his wife is deceased.

Feb 3 1936   Stanley Corbin[1]   Nethers VA

Mr JR lassiter dear mr lassiter i will write you a line Regarding a place
i would like to go one i would like to occypy the Walter Nichalson place

as Soone as He moves out He Have Rented a place at Brightwoode and planes to move Some time next month and His place would Bee more Hander to my work as i Have a Summer Jobe as I am gote fether to walk then any of them that ar working one the Same jobe it is So unhandy up Hear for a doctor the doctor Said He was Not coming no whar only whar He could get in His car it is So lonsom one my wife When i am at worke in Site and Hearing of nobody So Plese Sind me a letter to occypy the Place when He gets aute Yours veary truly ancer at once

1. Stanley Corbin was married to Polly Nicholson, who was John T. Nicholson's sister and John Russ Nicholson's daughter. He moved to the home of Velt Nicholson (Polly's uncle) on tract 30 in Madison County. See also the letters of March 2, July 13, and November 28, 1936, and February 28, 1938.

~~~

Swift Run, Va.   Feb. 14, 1936.

Mr. Cammere.

Kind sir: Just a few lines in regard to the Park land as I am living inside the park. I have very small place on the outside Boundary line on both sides of the Spottswood trail. My buildings are very old. House and stable are about 75 years old. I signed up for my place and I have tried to take care of it just as it was whhen I am going to move out and when I move out if they do as usual it will be robbed anyway. And I am asking you if I can have any of my buildings. I have one old building 10 × 16 planed logs, one building 6 × 10 dairy house; blacksmith shop 16 × 20. Just a hull no roof. Good roof on old barn. Roof is all.

I have got about two or three yards of wire fence and post lying on both sides of Spottswood trail. Joins no land at all. I would appreciate these if I can get any or all. I would move all and clean up old scraps and will there be any farming in park this year? Please let me hear from you at once, and thanking you.

Resp.

Joseph W. Baugher,[1]

Swift Run, Va.

As I am going out now soon if I move out now soon. If I move out windows, doors, roofing, fencing and all as here to fore, will be gone. If tore down by the CCC boys it is mostly all burnt up if I can get it honest I will appreciate it as I need it to build my little place I have got.

Thank you for your information.

1. Joseph Baugher owned eight acres on tract 83 in Rockingham County and was paid $1,935 by the state. Baugher explains to National Park Service director Arno Cammerer that in the process of his waiting for and moving to a homestead, the buildings on his property will probably be robbed. He requests that rather than have the buildings and their contents stolen or destroyed by the park, he be able to move the contents for his own use. His letter reflects what many residents were obliged to do as they moved. Since the buildings became park property, residents were not allowed to take any of the materials without permission from the government. Letters such as Baugher's illustrate that in the process of removal, residents were compelled to interact formally with these officials so that they could make the best use of the materials.

---

febury the 17 1936   Mr Andrew Nicholson   Nethers Va

halow mr lassiter
i are ritting you Just a few lins to see if you will let me have Mr Velt Nicholson house i heared that he is goin to move if he move could i have his house the reason i wants to move my house aint very good it do leak and Blow in snow and it is nearer to my work and it is nearer fore the children to go to chool and it is Better waie to the store that is the reasons i want to move it is a Better house will you please send me ritting fore the house and let me heare frome you at once frome Andrew Nicholson[1]

1. Andrew Nicholson lived in Madison County.

---

february 19 1936   Please excuse this Paper[1]
from WD Taylor   Skyland Va

Dear mr laseter i want to ask if we are to remain in they Park untill next fall as we live in Madison Co and they have not Prepard us a home yet if we are going to remain here till fall i want to ask you to rite me along this line just what we can depend on and i want to ask if you can give me some

work of some kind as i have not had much work since i were gate gard i
hope you may and can faind me somethig to do which i will thank you
verry much for what informitation you may give me along all this i want
to say not as i am medling with any of they Park afairs at all But i have
Bin infomed that some serten Parties has Bin fishing an white ake and
ather streams in they Park eria and have Bin using dinemite and as i learn
have caught hundreds ather ways and i though you aught to no this But
Please dont thing i am nedling with any at they Park afairs as i no it is
against they law to dinemite fish any where and at any time i shall let you
no of any violatians af they law that [several words unclear] in they Park
eria as i always take a Pride in saving they forest game and Birds and fish
for if we dont Protect this we will soon have none i hope to here from you
in a few days regarding aur vacating the Park i hope you and your family
and mr Zerkel family are all well and enjoying the Best of helth and also
all your office help

yours verry truly
W.D. Taylor,[2] skyland Va

1. Taylor's letter is written on Skyland Hotel stationery, with the heading crossed
through. Skyland was the mountain resort that was owned by George Pollock and
that was near where Taylor lived.

2. See also the letters of December 21, 1935; March 16, 1936; October 7 and 24,
1937; and January 24, 1938; and the letters by Bernie Lee Taylor, W.D.'s son, dated
October 12, 1935, and January 11, 1936.

<div align="center">~~~</div>

Swift Run, Va.   February 19, 1936.

Charles H. Taylor,
Washington, D.C.
Dear Sir:

I am liveing here in the park area way up in the mountain and the
House I am living in dont have but 3 room and it ant so good it hasn't got
a piece of plain lumber in it. Will you give it to me I sure would appreciate
it if you would do that much for me if you don't believe what I am writing
to you about this house you can write Mr. Bert and he can come and look
at the house and also they are a press built in the house to. some people
will go ahead and take the building and not ask you. But I wouldn't take

nothing like that and I am ask you for this building and I hope you will give it to me when we people move out of a park house they allway tear them down and burn them up outside of what people slip around and get. I believe you ought to give it to a poor person that I know I would if I was own it and I surely would be glad and appreciate it very much if you will give it to me.

Very truly yours,
Mrs. Rebecca Baugher,[1]
Swift Run, Va.

I was give information to you and if you are not the right man please hand it to right man and oblige.

Write me at once please.

1. Rebecca Jane Powell Baugher was the wife of Lloyd Baugher. The Baughers were tenants who lived near tract 36 in Rockingham County. See also the letters of May 8, 1935, and March 31, 1936.

<div style="text-align:center">~~~</div>

Swift Run, Va.,   Feb. 21 1936.

Mr. J. R. Lassiter

Dear Sir:—I beg the privelidge, that this plea for mercey will be given your attention. I have been living under false impression for some time to realize that I am now faceing a very serious problem. Some time ago a man representing him self as a man from your office came to my house. after asking and answering a few questions he told me he was signing me for a special permit. as he handed me the paper to sign. I ask that it be read. his reply was there are two sheets of this, I have so many places to go. and I want to get through to rush these in to the office. this dosent a mount to any thing only a few restrictions. I signed it. Mr Osbourn your Permit will be mailed to you from Luray. and hurridly left. in a few days he returned handing me a sheet of paper saying please sign this. then he handed me two sheets of paper saying this is your special permit to the first of April. I remarked what after April the first. Oh! things will be as they have been was his reply. after he left, I looked over the papers. and find that I had signed the same papers that he had when he was first here. and which was suppose to be mailed to me from your office. I made inquire to find out if every body was given the same permit that I had. and every one I asked said they had not received one. and was told that the reason I had this permit is because I was not signed up for a homestead. after I moved here I applied to Mr Carson that I might be signed for a homestead. He refered my letter to Mr Zirkle. He wrote me stating that no one was signed up after a certin date. that statement was false. for other people have moved in park property since I moved here. and they have been signed up for a homestead. Mr Lassiter I am not asking for special privedliges but may the same consiterations be granted to me as well as to others. I was living in the park area and just befor the land was purchased by the park. I lost everything I had by fire. a few people give me some things and I moved in a car shed. and on August the 31st 1934 this place was made vacant by J. Clyde Shifflett. and I moved in. just as other people did and have been doing as each place was made vacant. I wish to call your attention to this <u>sad</u>[1] fact. that if I am compelled to abide by this so called permit that my wife and our little 4 year old baby boy and myself will have to face the cold dark world with no where to go. I am an American borned citizen, Also law a biding, have been for a number of years an Evangelist preacher but owing to Ill health and other misfortunes I am left in a very poor condition. there is no one in this part of the park area that is in the condition that I am in. ponder these words. that if I am forced to vacate April the first. those that will remain. some of them have money enough to buy and will buy farms when they will have to vacate the park. others have all ready purchased homes. with their money they got for their park land. and while my family and my self. may be out of doors. these people will be enjoying the hospitality of the park conservation. If I could remain here for a little while longer. I could be in better circumstances. this is an out of the way place and the old house is in its last decay. it is with in your power to grant me an extention of time will you be so kind as to do it. It is appointed to every man once to die. we do not know what might befall us. be for death over takes us. I pray that God will bless you, and your future life. I am closing, hoping that this plea for mercey will find favor in your reply. I am yours truly.

H. R. Osbourn
Swift Run Va

1. The word "sad" is underlined three times.

Febuary 24 1936

Dear Mr lassater
I wood like to move in another house that Wavely L. Dyer[1] owned. it
would Be closer to Scool for the children and closer to the farming land
that I have a Permit to farm and I would like to take the windows and
Doors and wire from the house I now ocuppy I would like to no if it would
Be all Rigt to make the exchange Please Let me no By Return mail
    adress Charles C. Dyer
    Syra Va
Please let me no at once So I can move

   1. Waverly Dyer owned 225 acres on tract 94 in Madison County and was paid
$1,130 by the state.

Feb 24 1936

Dear Sir
Mr J.R. Lassiter
I am writing you a few lines to day as I would like to no if I can rase any
thing this coming year and theys a pice of land here that had wheat on
about 2 years ago and theys nothing but weeds on it and I would like to
no if I can plow it for you no I have got to have sum thing to eat and I
want your concent before I do any thing for if it had not been for what I
rased my fimily would haved straved this winter and I want you to do all
you can for me I writin to Mr Zerkel sum time ago about the land and cuting sum dead Lockus wood and I never heard any thing from him about
either wone and he must not a got my letter for he has been good to me
and so good I jus dont know how good he has been he all ways lets me no
about any thing I ask him about this place and I feal that you will do the
same I would like for you a Mr Zerkel will com and sea me when the
weather gets perty

                                          Yours very truly
                                          Robert Matthews[1]
                                          Bentonville Va

1. See also the letters of December 16, 1935, and January 1, March 29, and May 26, 1937, and the letter written by Mrs. Robert Matthews dated September 6, 1936.

~~~

Swift Run Va   Feb 26, 1936

Dear sir

As it is nearly time to plant garden. I am writing to know if I can stay in the park another year if so please let me know as I sined for a Homestead I would like to plant some things. As I havent got much place to plant any thing here. I am asking the permision to plant the patches on Ambros Shifflets place. As Melvin Hansbrough has done moved out of the park area. He lived on Ambros place. Mr Charles Davis burnt part of the fence around my garden. and also cut lots of green timber also some cherry trees so please let me here from you at once

<div align="right">
Yours Truly
Otis L. Davis[1]
</div>

1. Davis requested in his January 26, 1935, letter that he be allowed to move to the Charles Davis property, tract 181 in Rockingham County. Otis Lee Davis was the husband of Helen Mae Baugher, daughter of Lloyd L. and Rebecca Jane Powell Baugher. See also the letters of May 8, 1935, and February 19 and March 31, 1936.

~~~

March: 1 1936   Swift Run, Va.

Dear Sir

I Been told That i could stay here tell Fall I live close To The Ilas Place where Ambous Shiflett move frome I Just like to See if I could farm The garden If no body else had not Got it

Yours Truly
Boss Morris[1]

1. See also the letters of January 14, February 26, and March 10, 1935.

~~~

March 2 1936   Stanley Corbin Nethers Va

Mr JR Lassiter dear Mr lassiter i gote your letter to move in the Walter Nicholson House i Rather move in the WB Nicholson House as it is

Letter from Madison County resident Stanley Corbin to James R. Lassiter, March 2, 1936. (Courtesy of Shenandoah National Park Archives; used by permission of Corbin's family)

amuch Better place He is going to move out in afew days So now plese Sind me a letter for His place as i dont want to kick up no truble Buck dodson says He is going to move in Walter Nicholson House So plese Sind me one at once So i can move in as He moves oute i will wright you Soone as i move mr lassiter i was informed the other day By Hary Jenkens that you wanted a man to look after the Nicholson Hollar River to pervent peple from fishing if this Bee true i would Bee glade of that jobe So if you want me to look after it Rite and let me now give me full infomation about it So ancer at once

yours very truly

Stanley Corbin[1]

1. See also the letters of February 3, July 13, and November 28, 1936, and February 28, 1938.

~~~

Skyland, Va.   March 3, 1936

Mr J. R. Lassiter.
Luray, Va.
Dear Sir:
I am going to tell you how the people down in Nicholson Hollow is cuting
green wood. Dennis Corbin has been cutting green wood. and Luther
Corbin has been cutting down green apples trees burning them. and Velt
Nicholson also has been cutting green wood and has been selling it with
dry wood out of the park. and Walter Nicholson and Buddy Nicholson
and Rast Nicholson has been doing the same [line missing] wiskey and
selling it. and on friday and Saturday is their main days to boot leg their
wiskey and sell it to the work men on the PWA. I think it is against the
park Rules to make and sell whiskey in the park. and they are boasting
that they dont have to buy goverment whiskey that they can make it on
their awn. and selling it to the men that is working on the PWA that
needs money for their fashilys. and Dinnis Corbin has a 100 bushels of
apples yet and would not give his neighbers any and they are all frays and
he is sellig them yet. if you doubt my word send some one and see unex-
eptdly. also stanley corbin makes wheskey. Now you can send some one
and let them see for themselves if my statements are not true. Please dont
haul my name in this but if you will keep quiet and send ar go yourself it
wont be long till you will haul some of them

yours truly.
Mrs. Fanney Corbin[1]

1. Fanney Corbin was married to Charles W. "Buck" Corbin, who owned fifty-six
acres on tract 35 in Madison County and was paid $845 by the state. Like several
other residents, Fanney Corbin reported her neighbors' activities because park officials had become the law enforcement in the area. James Luther and Dennis Corbin
were Fanney's brothers-in-law. See also the letter of June 22, 1937.

Nethers, Va.   March 3, 1936

JR Lassiter
    Dear Sir
Buddie Nicholson is talking About moving from the Park area. Will it be
all right for me to move in if he moves out because my house roof is bad
and that one is better. will it be all right for the gardens here and also the
ones at Buddie Nicholson and the Fruit: Could you give me the job looking after the rivers and game. It is people over her that will fish & hunt &
trap. infiance of the law. We haven had any more fire since I caught those
two fire bugs last spring I realy broke up that. and I think if I had the job
I could stop that hunting I will appreciate it if I can get the job I will do
my best to catch

Sincerely yours
J Luther. Corbin[1]

1. See also the letter of June 18, 1935.

March the 5 1936   Oldrag Va

Dear Mr Lassiter just a Few Lines to ask you iF i Can tend the garden at
Mr W A Brown he has dun LeFt the park and there is a Few apples trees
there Can i have them this year the Road Came throug my garden and i
am close to that garden i wood Like to tend that iF i Can i am a Widow
and i haFt to work So hard please Let me no at once yours truly

Mrs John R Nicholson[1]

i have home Sted papers

1. Elizabeth Corbin Nicholson, who was John T. Nicholson's mother. John "Russ"
Nicholson died December 16, 1935.

~~~

Fletcher, Va   Mch 7 / 36

Mr L. Ferdinand Zerkel
Luray, Va
Dear Sir—

If it meets with your approval, I would like to move from my place into the house the Park bought from my Mother, Mrs Ardista Lamb. There's no one looking after this place and I could look after the Box wood and take care of it until Mr Carson removes it. You see I have to give up my place after this year. Have permit to stay this year. I prefer to move into my mother's house if it is all right with the Park authorities. Please let me know about just as soon as you possible can. I would like to move soon as possible on account of planting out garden.

yours Truly
James Lamb[1]
Fletcher,
Greene Co. Va

1. James Lamb owned twenty-eight acres on tract 10 in Greene County and was paid $490 by the state. See also the letter of April 27, 1936, and the letter written by Lamb's mother, Ardista, dated September 7, 1935.

~~~

Elkton, Va   Mar. 9, 1936   Rt. 1,

Dear Sir.

May I get some dead wood off the place where I moved from for my own use. I will appreciated it if I could. I moved out of the park November 8, 1934 and didn't cause you all any trouble. Answer at once.

Your truly,
From Victoria Meadows Hensley[1]

1. Victoria Meadows Hensley was married to Thomas N. Hensley, who owned twenty acres which were on tract 8 in Rockingham County and on tract 692 in Page County, which were not purchased. Victoria owned 215 acres on tract 643 in Page County and on tract 1 in Rockingham County. Of those 215 acres, 28 were purchased by the state for $86.

Swift Run Va.   March 10 1936

JR Lassiter.

Dear Mr Lassiter

I am writing you to know if you will give me permission to farm the piece of land which Mr Jessie Sims farmed last year on the Alex Haney track. It is not near the Drive, ar Highway ar in sight of any scenery. Mr Sims has moved out side the Park area, Mr Haney is also moving. If you will permit me please let me hear from you once. Very Respectfully yours

Sam Shiflett[1]

Swift Run Va.

1. In a March 20, 1936, letter, Shifflett asked if he could move to the Alex Haney tract in Greene County.

March 13 1936   Nethers Va

dear Mr Lassiter i Want you to let me farm a Bout 2 ackers of land on Hilton Nicholson place the land have not got no grass on it Nothing But some Brils Jemmil Dodson is farming some Just like it so let me hear from you at Wonce from

EB Nicholson[1]

Nethers Va.

1. Ephraim B. Nicholson, Lillie Pearl Nicholson's father. See also the letters of April 4 and 18 and May 1, 1938.

March 16, 1936

Dear Mr lasiter

i want to ask if we are going to Be left in the Park eria untill fall as it is getting late now and is time we were fixeing to make garden and to Plant aur ather Crops untill we can get ready it will Be time to Plant some garden stuff and we will Be glad to stay until fall and will ast you to Please rite me in regard to all this and i will ask you as soon as it Be so you will

give me that Job as i shure will Be glad to get a Job which i will thank you
i hope you and all your family are all and enjoying the Best of helth give
my Best regards to mr zircl and family mr laseter if i am given a Job in
this Park eria and given they rite and Power i shure will do my Best in
every way to Protect every thing to my Best ability as i always have taken
a Pride an looking after they will fair at aur forest game ànd Birds and fish
and every thing elce so i hope you may reches me and give me something
to do in they near futher

yours verey truly
WD Taylor[1]
skyland Va

1. Like Taylor's letter of February 19, 1936, this letter is also written on Skyland
stationery. See also the letters of December 21, 1935; February 19, 1936; October 7
and 24, 1937; and January 24, 1938.

〜〜〜

Mar. 16, 1936

Dear Mr. Lassiter:

I am living on the old Sinpton place and I signed a home stead special
permit and will you please tell me if I can stay on ar not I would like to
stay this year as I have Wheat on the place and I am 77 years old and have
a wife and 4 children to take care of and I have been able to find a Place to
go thay say you are agoing to leave the house stand and I Will take care
of the house I have been here a long time and would like to stay the rest
of my day here and I Will help to fix in thing to keep the Place up I see
some people have Just moved in a house right here last year so please let
me know at once as I wont to make a harden some one told me that you
would let me stay the reast of my days but I would like to know from you
so I could rest I am getting old now to have to move please let me know
at once

Very turely yours
R.C. Fox[1]
Front Royal Va

1. Richard Calvin Fox. See also the letter of December 26, 1936.

Swift Run Va.   March 20 1936

Dear Mr Lassiter

I am writing you in regards to Mr Alex Haneys house, I saw Mr Bert about it and he said I would have to write you will you allow me to move in that house after he moves He is moving now and says he will finish by the 31 of Mar. As I have had to store my property at Mrs. Baughers. The house is not large enough to take care of all, I have some packed in the barn and it is very open. I would be glad to have the house. Please let me know

Very Respectfully yours
Sam Shiflett.[1]

1. See also the letter of March 10, 1936.

March 23 1936

JR lassiter i am writen to you to find out weather i can get them apples This year on the Place where i live at on PreancherS it is on the Park land up on the mouton i am taking care of the Place and i think it is Right fear me to get the apples this year i am looking out fear the place and taking care everthing and Promney [H. W. Pomeroy] got the apples last year and he didn do nothing to the orched and i have look after the orched and i think i ought to have the apples this year on the place So you write and let me no and all So i want to on about the garden and Patches all So and weather it will Be all Right to farm what i did last year. So Please let me no at once From

John Jewell[1]
Browntown Va

1. See also the letter of August 8, 1935.

~~~

Swift Run, Va.   March, 23, 1936.

Mr. Lassiter.
    Dear Sir.
    i am writeing to you as it is time to plow my garden and patches and i
aint heard any thing from you about it. and it is time to plow now when it
get dry—you try to answer at once.

                                                            yours truley
                                                        Clark. Shifflett.[1]
                                                        Swift Run. Va.

1. Clark Shifflett's mother, Barbara Ada Shifflett, owned fourteen acres on tract
192, and his father, Trice Shifflett, owned sixteen and a quarter acres on tract 191,
both in Rockingham County. Both tracts were surveyed, but neither was purchased
by the state. Clark's cousin John Henry Shifflett owned sixty-three acres on tract
132 in Rockingham County and was paid $1,634 by the state.

~~~

Mar. 24, 1936

Mr. J.R. Lassiter
Luray, Va.
Dear Mr. Lassiter—
    I am Writing to ask about plowing for a corn crop. Last year I put in
part of a field. This year I contemplate cropping the entire field with corn.
There being no set sod on this field. Why I ask you about this is some
folks here say I can't do this. And most likely report this to you.

                                                        Yours very truly,
                                                        Buck Dodson[1]

1. James Walker "Buck" Dodson requests in this letter that he be able to plow his
property for a corn crop. Because of the changeover in authority, many residents
were unsure whether plowing or harvesting was still allowable under the park's regulations. Indeed, the park officials' letters to residents indicate some discretion over
permissions granted, so many residents wrote letters like this one to ask formally
for permission to continue with their day-to-day living. See also the letters of September 8, 1936, and November 8, 1951 (the latter in the epilogue, on p. 161).

Swift Run, Va   March 25, 1936

J.R. Lassiter,
Luray Virginia
  Dear Sir;
  Mr R. Taylor Hoskins was up here to see me yesterday. I cut a few
trees when that deep snow and cold time was, I would not have done it,
But I was about to freeze in the house and I could not get any where els to
get any wood and I had to do this or freeze in the house as the snow was
so deep I could not hardley get to my Barn to feed I am real sorry I cut
them and I will not cut anymore Please Remember I am a old man 84
years old and to think what a winter we had and man my age had to get
wood from some where to keep from freezing and Remember I have never
give the park people no trouble, I have always done ever thing they said
                                                      Your Truly,
                                                      Charles Davis.[1]

  1. Charles Davis owned 151 acres on tract 181 in Rockingham County and was
paid $4,222 by the state.

March the 26 1936

  Mr. J. R Lassiter
  Dear Sir I am writing you to find out if I can put Ben Hensley and family out from here and if you will help me if I cant get them out my self?
Please sir write me up a vacation [eviction] notice that I can have served
on them to get out of the house that I am occupying now. let me hear from
you real soon
                                                      Mrs N. W. Hensley[1]
PS. I am being treated so bad I just cant stand it and stay here they are staying here under my permit you ask me to stay and take care of the house

  1. Columbia Frances Hensley was the wife of Nicholas Wysong Hensley. N. W.
Hensley owned 138 acres on tract 72 in Rockingham County and was paid $10,410
by the state. A handwritten note on Columbia Hensley's letter says, "B.F. Hensley
notified to vacate the residence of Mrs. N.W. Hensley."

~~~

Nethers Va   March 26 1936

Mr. J. R. lassiter
dear Sir i am writeing you to know if you would care if i would use the
logs that is in the old Barn for fire wood and give some to my neighbors
the wind has blowed it down and it ant any lumber in it i know you would
not care but i think it would be best to ask you i hope to hear from you at
once

<div align="right">

Yours truly
R. Velt Nicholson[1]

</div>

1. R. Velt Nicholson owned thirty-one acres on tract 31 in Madison County and
was paid $530 by the state.

~~~

March 27, 1936

Mr. J.R. Lassiter
Luray, Virginia
Dear Mr. Lassiter,
    I am writing you to know if we can handle the orchard in the park
land three miles east of Browntown, known as the Wines and Pomeroy
Orchard. I see Mr. Ikes has appointed you supertendent of the park, therefore I am taking this opportunity to ask you if you can grant us permission for same. I would appreciate it very much if you can arrange for us to
take care of the fruit. I am,

Sincerely yours,
H.W. Pomeroy [signed]
Wines and Pomeroy
By H.W. Pomeroy[1]

1. This letter is typed on H. W. Pomeroy stationery. See also the letter of February 26, 1935.

Swift Run Va.   March. 30 1936

Mr. J.R. Lassiter: Supt.

Luray, Va.

Dear Mr. Lassiter.

I am writing you in re-gard to a garden, from which I moved. my place
adjoins this small garden and I moved when I was notified to do so, & I
have not had time to fix my garden at home. I would appreciate your kindness if you would let me tind the garden this year.

I am a widow with three children to take care of

So please let me hear from you at once in re-gard to same.

Hope to hear a favorable reply.

Yours truly.

(Mrs.) Mitt Shifflett[1]

Swift Run. Va

1. Mrs. Mitt Shifflett lived in Rockingham County.

Swift Run Va   Mar 31, 1936

Mr. J R. Lassiter.

Luray Virginia

Dear Sir:

I wrote to Mr. charlie H. Taylor at Washington and He said the home
stead was divison at Luray. The house I live in is 3 small room and they
are not one piece of it plain lumber all rough it back Here in the High top
mountain and you cant get up Here with a truck nor a wagon you just
haftn slide it out would you be kind enough to give me this little Building
when the people move out of the park. up in Here what people dont slip
around and get the CCC boy burn it up and I hope you Had rather give it
to me then for Them to burn it up. I wouldn't go ahead and take thing and
not ask you all for them. I wish you could come back Here and see where
we live I bleive you would certianly give this Building if you dont believe
I live up here in this mountian. Just like I am writing to you you just write
and ask Mr. Bert I save the window out of one house for Mr Bert. I wrote

and told Him and He said He was coming and get them. My Husband was a Vutirn in the World War and He never has got a thing Well I will close Hope you will make up you mine to give me this Building as ever.

Your Truly

Mrs. Lloyd Baugher[1]

Swift Run, Va

answer at once.

1. Rebecca Jane Powell Baugher. See also the letter of February 19, 1936, and her husband's letter of May 8, 1935. The Baughers' daughter, Helen Mae, married Otis Lee Davis. See Davis's letter of February 26, 1936.

~~~~

<div align="center">
Syria Va   April 2, 1936
</div>

Dear sir

Just few lines to ask favor of you. Will give me a permit to my orchard which sold to the Park, That is at least enough for family use of the fruit that may grow there this year as there is no one living on the place; I always rather ask permission for fruit enough for home use now I will close with man thanks for your good will the past

<div align="right">
your's truly

Rosa Dyer[1]
</div>

1. Rosa Dyer was married to Herbert W. Dyer, who owned sixteen acres on tract 97 in Madison County and was paid $233 by the state. The land was surveyed as having fifteen peach trees. Rosa Dyer's phrase "for family use" comes from the park's special use permit, which allowed people to gather enough fruit from their property for their families only; this provision was intended to prevent people from collecting fruit and selling it for profit.

~~~~

April 7 1936   Stanley Va. R.1

Mr Lasenter

If Im to stay on the Park Ill have to farm the ground that is already cleared can John Offenbacker come and farm all the land that I have to farm he dont live on the Park land I wish you would notfy him to stay off of the park or the land that I have to farm and also Ernest Thomas he said

he were comig to farm on the Park if he wants to farm why cant he farm
at home on the Place where he lives I dont see where they have got any
rite to come and farm all the land that I have to farm so its up to you I
have told them that they could not farm all the land that I had but they
say they are going to farm it any way

Yours truly
Ben Meadows[1]
Stanley Va R1

1. Ben Meadows, Hiram M. Meadows's son, lived in Page County. See also the letter of February 7, 1938, and Hiram's letter of November 12, 1936.

April 8 1936   Oldrag Va

Dear Mr lassiter
Dear Sir I am writing you to get the permit for Mr hebert Dyer place
which he has moved out of the park for last year it was a lot of fruit there
last year and I did not get any of it So I would like to have the permit for
that orchard for this year

Mr. Charley E Dyer[1]
Oldrag Va

1. Charles E. Dyer owned sixty-four acres on tract 99 in Madison County and was
paid $717 by the state. His land was surveyed as having twenty-six apple trees. See
also the letters of April 10, 1936; November 5, 1937; and March 14 and August 12,
1938; and the letter of his wife, Lizzie Nicholson Dyer, dated May 8, 1936.

April 10, 1936   Syria Va

Mr lassiter dear sir I am sorry to tell you the house ie wrote to you about
we cant move ien the floore is all out some one tore it out and ie have no
lumber to fin it with so please give me apermission to tend where ie am
at and to get some fruit for family youse last fall ie did not get no apples
every Body got all of them and let them all rot and ie have the Bigest family of iny one around here
  so please let me no soon[1]

1. This letter is not signed. However, the letter is filed in the Charley Dyer folder in the park's archives and contains similar handwriting to Charley Dyer's other letters. See also the letters of April 8, 1936; November 5, 1937; and March 14 and August 12, 1938; and the letter of his wife, Lizzie Nicholson Dyer, dated May 8, 1936.

~~~

William Z Lam[1]   April 17 1936

mr Zerkel der sur i want to ask you for a pach i wanted to plant las year i roled of some rock las year an i never got to see you to ask for it an i got a few bushes of on it an i under stand by nabers that emit is going to plow my pach this year an thare is a pach of grss that grows very tall an i cut some on it last year an emit is going to plow it up an i dont want you to let him we are good frends you nead not tell i said any thing about that grass that is anew kind of grass an i dont want it plowd up emit has plowed mor grond than he could farm last year an now is going to plow mine iff you tell him not to plow up that grass dont[2] mention my name we are good frends tell me if i can plow my pach emit is got mare then he can manedge iff you dont want me to plow my pach pleas tell let me no at once i am going to clean the bushes out of that grass iff emit dont plow it up it grows four feet high it is anew kind of grass

  let me no soo dont tell emit he would git mad
  Route #1
  Elkton, Va

1. William Z. "Zebb" Lam owned thirty-five acres on tract 540 in Page County.
2. The word "dont" is written in larger letters than the rest of the letter.

~~~

April 27, 1936

Mr Lassiter I am writing to you in regard to Mr Roy taylor grzing his cows in the Park Land He is now grazing in the place that my mother Lives on Ardista Lamb Aand they give me trouble At times he lives out Side of the park and I wish you would atend to this

Yours truly
James Lam[1]
fletcher
Va

1. See also Lam's letter of March 7, 1936 (where he spells him name "Lamb"), and his mother's letter of September 7, 1935.

~~~

Sperryville Va   May 1936

Dear Mr Lassiter—

I am writing you to let you know we are now moving, there is a man watching the house each day he comes to see if we are out we have most all inside furniture out but have a lot out side to get yet so I would say you had better watch for this man moving in after tomorrow (Fri. Let me know when the building I ask you want be up for sale and do your best for me getting it will surley appreciate your kind deeds in doing so.

<div align="right">

Resp.

Lucile Ramey[1]

</div>

1. Lucille Ramey was James W. Ramey's daughter. James owned 219 acres on tracts 153 and 167 in Rappahannock County and was paid $10,609 by the state. See James's letters of November 30, 1935, and May 1936.

~~~

[no date but probably before May 1936]

Mr JR Lassiter
Luray Va
Dear Mr Lassiter,

want to tell you my wife is very sick Dr. comes ever day. would have moved this week had it not been for that. will move out just as soon as possible.

Thanking you,

Resp

Jas. W. Ramey[1]

1. See also the letter of November 30, 1935, and the letter of James's daughter, Lucille Ramey, dated May 1936.

Oldrag Va   May 1 1936

Mr. Lassiter

Dear Sir

Harry Berry is moving out the park to Pennsluvinia and how about me
moving in that house the house I am living in is all to pices almost it leaks
so bad con hardly find a dry place in the house when it rains and it ant
going to be no fruit where I live this time and like to get the fruit at that
Place answer reel soon

Yours truly

Davis Louis Dyer

[received May 7, 1936]

Dear Mr Lassister i Live in the Park near Oldrag Va and Wood Like to
have the Place that Mr Harrie Berry is Leaving there is apples there and a
good house the house i am in Verry Sorry So he will Leave next week So
please Let me move you write me a permet For the place until the home
Steds are Redy So please Mr Lassiter Let me have the place and Let me no
at once your truly

Mrs John R Nicholson[1]

Oldrag va

1. Elizabeth Corbin Nicholson. See also the letter of March 5, 1936, and the letters of her son, John T. Nicholson, dated September 11, 1935, and January 28 and
September 20, 1937.

May 8 1936   skyland Va

Dearst Mr R Taylor

Will you plese come Down and git ada Dodson to put His Hogs up aer
Drop Him a letter we Been wating all the spring and He want put them
up We hovent put out a Bit of girden yet they aer [are] sraying the green
zaud Dawn [down] Here we aer Both living on the zame Farm you come

Dawn at once if you come Dawn I want to zee you about a little pese of
grown I want to tend and let me no if I ante got the zame write to git apples on this place as well as ada Dodson and if you Dont come Dawn plese
Drope me a letter at zkyland Va

Mrs. Charley Dyer[1]
zkyland Va

1. Lizzie Nicholson Dyer. Dyer consistently wrote the letter *s* as "z." See her husband's letters of April 8 and 10, 1936; November 5, 1937; and March 14 and August
12, 1938.

Luray, Va.   June 2, 1936.

President Roosevelt,
Washington, D.C.
Dear Sir:

I am writing to you for information concerning the Homesteads for
the people who live in the Shenandoah Natl. Park, near Luray, Va. I live
at Panorama Hotel where I was caretaker last winter. The Hotel wont
run any more so I am out of a job there but if I understood the rules of the
Park right those that signed up for a Homestead had the privilege to stay
until they were finished. Mr. Lassiter is superintendent here I know but
he is disobeying park rules if I understand them right. He gave me notice
to get out by the last of the week so I wish you would write to me in reply
by return mail, telling me whether I have the privilege to stay or not. I
am a poor man with no job now or none in sight. I just cant find a job
nowhere. I am a wiling worker and am willing to do anything. I am not
choicey at all. I have a family to take care of that's all I am worrying
about. I can't care for myself but "God Bless My Family." I am hoping you
can help me and I am sure you would if you could see what a bad shape I
am in. Answer just as soon as you can because if you cant' help me I will
have to make other plans.

Very truly yours,
Charles T. Middleton,[1]
Luray, Va.
c/o Panorama Hotel.

1. Charles T. Middleton was the caretaker at the Panorama Hotel, located near Luray, Virginia. The Panorama Hotel was owned by J. Allen Williams, Paul Taylor, R. L. Cheatham, and A. M. Priest. The survey by the SCCD appraised the land and hotel at $16,987. See Janney-Lucas, "Why Not Panorama?" Charles T. Middleton is the only living letter-writer in this collection.

~~~

July 13 1936   Stanley Corbin[1]   Nethers Va

dear mr lassiter i will wright you about the apples one the J. M. Jenkins track witch you Belded to me last year i dinten get what of them i could use for family use last year. for Jimy dodsons family Stealing them and Stiling them So Plese wright and tell me if i can keep them from taking my apples as it ant no more then i will need if it is more i will vide them with my frind So ancer at once

yours truly

1. See also the letters of February 3, March 2, and November 28, 1936, and February 28, 1938.

~~~

Syria Va   July 18 1936

Dear Mr Lassiter:

I want a little information and I know you can give it. Here it is—If a party sells land to the Park above a fence, and to me below the fence. The fence not being exactly on the line all the way. some places it is from one foot to six feet on the park. Can the party that sold the land still claim that fence and move it away. he pastures in the park, and if he moves the line fence his cattle will come in on me: He says I will have to build a new fence now will I? He never mentioned this until I paid for the land: and he had been using that fence as a line fence 'till he sold below it, now is he intitled to the fence, please let me know at your earliest convenience.

Yours truly

Ida O. Lillard[1]

Syria Va

P.S. If it is your fence, will you let me use it for a line fence?
    Please do,
    Ida Lillard

1. Ida Lillard owned sixty-four acres on tract 114 in Madison County and was paid $1,236 by the state.

~~~

Whitehall, Moormans River, Va.   July 27, 1936.

Mr. J. R. Lassiter, Supt.
  Shenandoah National Park
  Luray, Va.
Dear Sir;

For the past ten years I have been living in the dwelling house on Major Rollers land located on the North Fork of Moormans River within Shenandoah National Park. Last winter I left my residence spending the winter with my brothers family at Harriston, Va. and moving back into my house this spring. Since then I have planted several truck patches which I would like to harvest and therefore request that you kindly permit me to occupy my house during the remainder of the year.

I am 52 years of age, wife deceased, two children living in Harriston.

As I was not living in the park when the Special Use Permits were issued last winter, I do not have one.

Very truly yours,
ED BOWEN[1]

1. The Roller tract was in Albemarle County, tract 128. See also the letter of November 20, 1936, and Polly Bowen's letter of February 1, 1936.

~~~

8/8 1936[1]

Hon Harry F. Byrd
  Dear Sir

I had an order from Camp No 10 for Some apples drove up there with the apples & delived quantity bargained for at 100 for Bus fourty Sumed were perused & went to Camp No 1 & some one halted me well dressed & told Mr Sill this camp if they would buy not go any further as was violation of rule operate truck on the road when other trucks bring in apples Said four city truck Richmond and making price 12d for applies is price thear.

Is possible that officers in linc withe city man for the purpose of making hand on the produces

Can you give me Some information who to write to in regard the matter Thanking you in advance

Yours as ever

JW Nethers

PS what are these folks at the Camp gong to live on if no trucks are allowed to haul in the apples

1. This letter is written on Nethers Orchard stationery. James W. Nethers was the proprietor of this apple orchard. He owned 151 acres on tract 18 in Madison County and 18 acres on tract 250 in Rappahannock County and was paid a total of $1,354 by the state.

Skyland, Va.   august 10—1936

Mr R. Taylor Hoskins
Luray, Va.
My Dear Mr Hoskins.
Just a few lines regarding the fencing wire at camp No 3 which you said you would get if I needed it. I would be very glad if you could get it for me. Hoping to see you soon an hear from you.
I Remain

Resptfully Yours,

Richard Nicholson[1]

1. See also the letters of November 11, 1935, and August 7, 1945 (the latter in the epilogue, on pp. 159–60), and the letters written by Richard's mother, Teeny Florence Corbin Nicholson, dated December 29, 1934, and March 8 and 26, April 13, and August 7, 1938.

september 6 1936   Bentonville

dear sir:
i no where there is a Big apple archart on Back on the mounten from where we lived But it is on the Park land on the same trail i heard aBout it long ago and i ask the Boys that work Back there and they told me it was there and there were lots of apples and we ant got ane this year and i want to no if i can go Back there and get me what i need for my own use as we ear Bad in need this year has Ben a year that there isent much rained we

had plenty last year but we ant got it this year will you Please let me no at once if i can get the apples i no some one will get them if i cant so write away it will not Be no use to go and anather thing i want to ask you my son found a Bee tree and i want to no if we can cut it i Believe it has a lot of honey in it and it shore would come in for us so Please let me no By return mail and i will thank you so much sincrly

                                                                        Mrs Robert Matthews[1]

I lived on the J i Morgan farm on the mounten well i guess this will be our last year i guess we cant stay no longer i hate to think of it i like here so well it is a good place

1. Rubie C. Matthews. See also Robert Matthews's letters of December 16, 1935; February 24, 1936; and January 1, March 29, and May 26, 1937.

Sept 8 1936   Nethers Va

Dear Mr Laster

will you plese let me have some apple down hear in Velt Nicholson archers below the old baarn it ant got no feince around it. I have asked the force ranger for them but he did not come down hear. We have not got no apples round my house. The cows is running in the archers and write an tell me if I can have them. Velt have got his yard full of apples in we got none. Will you plese siend the force ranger down hear.

                                                                        Mr Buck Dodson[1]

I am up on Skylian at work you send ranger up hear an tell me. in send me a note to get them

1. See also the letters of March 24, 1936, and November 8, 1951 (the latter in the epilogue, on p. 161).

October 23, 1936

Secretary Ickes[1]
Washington, D.C.
Dear Sir:

    I have been picking apples on the DeJarnett farm for several years until it was sold to the park. Now I want to ask your permission to let me go there and get some apples to make apple butter and for fruit is very scarce. If I can get some from there please write and let me know at once. Hoping to hear from you soon.

Resp.

John W. Lamb, March, Va.[2]

1. This letter is typed, probably by the office assistant of Secretary of the Interior Harold Ickes. The DeJarnette Orchard was on thirty-two acres on tract 43 in Greene County.
2. John Wesley Lamb. See also the letter of November 5, 1936.

<div align="center">~~~</div>

Oct. 26. 1936   Nethers Va.

Mr J. R. Lassiter
Dear friend will you Please give me the old lumber here in the House where i am living i have bought me a small farm and the House on it is not comfortable to live in and i just connot buy new lumber to fix up my House i would very thankful to you. Mr Lassiter could you send two trucks Here to move my Property for me i am not able to Hire any i want to move in a bout 35 days i will move close to Madison. Can you send some men Here and tear down the House once i move let me no if i can move this old lumber before you tear it down i rote you a few days a go hope to hear from you by return mail

yours truly,

W.B Nicholson.[1]

1. William B. "Buddy" Nicholson owned twenty-one acres on tract 24 in Madison County and was paid $976 by the state. See also the letter of November 20, 1937.

<div align="center">~~~</div>

March, Va   Nov 5, 1936

Mr. J.R. Lassiter
Luray, Virginia
My dear Mr Lassiter:

I wrote to Arno B. Cammerer about some apple in the Park, and he suggested that I write to you. It is DeJarnette Orchard that I want to git soon apple from, for to use, because it is not any apple around that one can git to use. I picked the orchard two or three time before the park taken it over. I would like to hear from you at once.

Sincerely yours,
John W. Lamb.[1]

1. As Lamb's letter of October 23, 1936, suggests, he wrote to the offices in Washington, D.C., and was evidently referred to Lassiter to pose his request.

~~~

Nov the 6 1936   Nethers Va

Mr. J R Lassiter i am riting you this morn asking you can i move to the JR Nicholson Place—where Roosevelt Nicholson his son now lives—an he is getting ready to move out pretty soon an i would like to get that house for this winter as its more comfortable than mine an also it is down off of the mountain that is why i want it so bad for i am not able to go up an down the mountains much no more an my DR told me to never walk up er down the mountain but i cant do no beter if i ever go any where. i dont like to stay at home all the time an then too it is so hard on my husband an son too where works on the Ditch work at skyland they have this mountain to walk up an down ever nite & morn they have 6 or 7 miles to walk ever day going an coming at they work up there an you know that is harder on them than there work they do an my husband has bin at this work all the year an diden have no chance to put out no crop so we wont have no field to winter our stock on unless wages goes up Some so we will have something to buy with an then we cant get no one to have feed up this mountain we live on i was in good hopes at the Government would bin pd us for our little place long a go so we could bin looked us out a little home some where an bin moved to it bee fore bad weather sets in for we sure had a time geting in an out last winter so i trust at you will help me out in geting off this mountain for this winter by leting me move on to the house where Velt is going to leave so if i can have it you bee sure an tell them not to up set the house none er move none of the fence away from the place for i heard at they wer going to move all the lumber out of the house at they could get an if they do that why it woulden bee fit for any thing then so me & my husband has fully Decided to take us a Gov-

ernment home—long as we are not able to buy us no Place so at the Boys
could do the farming to make a living on it for us my husband has not bin
able to work none on this Dich job for over 3 week on acount of a bad soar
on his left hand an it sure has throwed us Back too he has bin to the DR—
4 times for it an may have to go 4 more times i do really think he ought to
have Pay for all this time he coulden work an his DR Bills bee Pd up too
as he never lost a day i dont think untill his hand stoped him i thought at
the Relief would help to keep people going at got sick an needed help
where has bin working on it for Serval years But we have never had a bit
of help in no way—all this year—an last year too only jest what my man
get out of his work i cant see why at most all the other men gets food orders ever mo [month] an clothes for the children an things for the Beds
an my Husband cant get nothing er my eldest son where is married dont
get nothing either only his mo. pay for his work so i hope if there is anything you can do to help me on this at you will for me an all the children is
in Bad need of clothes for the winter an i need things for my Beds also as
it takes what litle my Husband can make to keep the family in Bread &
feed the 2 Hogs so he hasent got nothing to buy the family nothing to
wear out of so Please do all you can for me & us some help for food an
clothes as we are in Bad need of those things an Please let me hear from
you at once—a bout this house i have asked you for—i will appreciate you
very much for your kindness of helping me out in time of need. Yours very
Respect

Mrs Jas Campbell[1]

1. Lillie Pearl Nicholson Campbell was married to James R. Campbell, who owned
forty-six acres on tract 247 in Rappahannock County, for which he was paid $1,057
by the state, and twenty-five acres in Madison County on tract 13, for which he was
paid $503 by the state. This is the first of several long letters (this one is fourteen
pages) written to Lassiter by the Campbells. Some of the letters that are signed
"James R. Campbell" or "Jas R Campbell" are written in the same handwriting as
those signed "Mrs. Jas R Campbell." This one is signed "Mrs. Jas R Campbell," but
the return letter written by Lassiter is addressed to Mr. James Campbell. Though
Lillie Campbell's letter states that she wants to move to John Russ Nicholson's
house (because her current house is far from her husband's work and from the doctor), that her husband is out of work due to an injury and has multiple doctor's bills,
and that her children are in need of clothes, Lassiter says in his reply only, "I regret
that it will be impossible to let you move there. It may be that I can move you to a
better house some time in the future." Lassiter gives no explanation, and although

Campbell's letter reflects a desperate and immediate need for her family, Lassiter's reply is vague as to when he might be able to help her. Many return letters are similar to Lassiter's in this case; the Park Service seemed ill-equipped to handle the various needs of mountain residents. Lillie Pearl Nicholson Campbell was William B. "Buddy" Nicholson's sister. See also the letters of November 22, 1936; August 18 and November 30, 1937; and January 8 and February 14, 1938.

~~~

11/12/36   Mr. J.R. Lassiter

Luray Virginia
Dear Mr Lassiter Would you Do me a favor if you Please I am going to ask of you To noty Alfred Meadows to keep his hogs off of my primisses he Lives In the Park and I Live out side and They have Burned the Fence and his hogs is coming down on my place Runing I [in] my grain and all over the Place and They will keep them off of my Place they come the Co Road all they way and it is possitively against The Law and If you Would write and ask him I think he will kick Them of all Write and Thank you very much

<div align="right">HM Meadows[1]
Elkton Va R1</div>

1. Hiram M. Meadows owned 132 acres on tract 554 in Page County, land that was originally surveyed but not purchased for the park.

~~~

Harriston. Va   11/20/36

My Dear Friend
i am writing to you about would you please give me a permit to stay on longer the weather is getting rough and colder and i have out a right smart crop and i dont have any where to go and i don't think I can hardly get out as soon as my permit is suspent and would you please give me more time

i would look after the timber and keep people from cutting any of it for you

So please answer at once and give me longer time if you please

Yours Truly
Ed. Bowen[1]

The permit i have ends January 1 1937
i live on the Major Roller track
Moormans River

1. See also the letters of February 1 and July 27, 1936.

Nov the 22nd 1936

Mr Lassiter

Dear Sir i appreciate your kindness in leting me Know now a bout me
moving to the JR Nicholson Place where i asked for i would bee very glad to
bee down off of this mountain as its so unhandy in an out so i hope you will
Provide a way for me to bee closier to my work an more handy to the stores
& schools as i have 2 children here at ought to bee in school ever day—an we
havent even got a school yet an if it was i coulden sind them when the
weather gets bad on acount of the mountain So i trust you will bee of great
help to me in the future yours very truly Mr & Mrs Jas Campbell[1]
PS—

also me an all my family are Destitute of clothes for the winter as i
never do get no food orders er clothes for none of my family like lots of
other People gets to help us out in no Respect an it takes what little earn-
ings at my Husband gets to buy Bread for the family an a few clothes for
his self i would highly appreciate it if you would see at i got some clothes
for the 2 Boys at is here at home with me yet as they need shoes an clothes
under wear an top clothes too they are 10–14 years old—so plase help me
if you can—as we are in bad need of help—Mrs Jas Campbell

1. James R. Campbell and Lillie Pearl Nicholson Campbell. See also the letters of
November 6, 1936; August 18 and November 30, 1937; and January 8 and
February 14, 1938.

Nov 28 1936   Stanley Corbin[1]   Nethers VA

Mr JR lassiter
dear mr lassiter i will wright you to let you know i am moving in the
House Velt Nicholson living in He wants us to take cear of His Stuff untell

He can move it all oute i dont want to Stay thar No longer then wee can Rent us a Place the House wee ar living in leeks So Bad it is So fair in and oute our doctor told us that He could Not come to See us No more tell wee moved out of Such a Place. i dont want to live whear a doctor cant come as i have two little childern Dry wood is so fair away Hear So you Plese Sind me a letter for the House as it is So much despute over it sirvel [several] familys wants to go in it So i can finish moving Mr lassiter Plese Sind my letter By Haywood taylor Monday yours veary truly

Stanley Corbin

1. See also the letters of February 3, March 2, and July 13, 1936, and February 28, 1938.

<div align="center">~~~~</div>

Dec. 5 1936   Swift Run Va

Dear Sir. I was informed by Mr. Smith at Camp 3[1] to write you about the T.B. Hensley Place here where I live. I have decided not to take a Home Stead. If I can get these old Buildings Here. I have a place in Ven. where I could use Some of these old logs & Boards here they have all about fallen down. It isent very much good, in all of it. If I Can get These old Buildings. I will Tear them all down & clean up the Place. Fences & all & Burn all the waste. Free of charg for what good is in them. & I will move in a Short time. You could have some body look the Place over. & see what good is in them.

Please let me know soon.

Yours very truly.
Elmer. Hensley[2]
Swift Run Va

1. "Camp 3" refers to the members of the Civilian Conservation Corps camp who were working on building Skyline Drive and other park projects.

2. See also the letter of May 19, 1934.

12.10.1936   R. 1. B. 246   Elkton Va

Dear sirs

In regard to the option on my place and dident take it. I don ever thing I Could do to get the park In the first place I gave 10 acres of land and went around with the men and showed them the cornors and did not receive a penny last winter the CC boys come and blasted my road full of rocks and went away. and left my road in such a bad shape we couldent get a doctor in the whole winter. and the children had to stop school as the buss could not get in. and this winter they have bin out of school a week on account of bad roads every family is close to the school but the ones living on the blue ridge mountain that have to go over this road some have haf to pay fines on account of the CC leaving the road in such a bad shape. asking you kindly to take my place for the next ones as we hafto meet the doctor about 2 miles on horse back I have don all I could to get the park thinking It would take my Place you no it has took all around me just leaves room for us to go out over the park. hope you will be kind enough to take it and help me that much as the children isent getting any learning. my road was in good shape until the CCC boys blasted It up that way the state has quit working the road. and the CCC has quit to and the Park has Knocked me out of sale for my place people dont want It on a count of the Park so please let me here from you please be kind enough to take my place so I can get out before so long thanking you to do me a favor and let me here from you all as soon as you can I remain as ever your friend

Mr B. H. Lam[1]

R1 B246

Elkton Va.

1. Bluford Henry Lam owned ninety acres on tract 4 in Rockingham County, land that was originally surveyed but not purchased for the park. Lam's letter reveals how residents called for the park administration's accountability in affecting their daily livelihoods.

Dora Corbin (Mrs.
Marvin "Woodie"
Corbin) and her son,
Austin, Madison
County residents.
(Courtesy of
Shenandoah National
Park Archives; used by
permission of Corbin's
family)

Dec. 26, 1936

Dear Mr Lassiter:

I have found a place to move but I can't get it until the last of Feb I have
had a time to find a place to go I would like to know if I can stay here until
I can get moved some of the people here are staying in the Park until
April 15 I wont to ask you before I stay I can get moved by that time I am
sure so please let me know.

Very truly your
R.C. Fox[1]
Front Royal Va

1. See also the letter of March 16, 1936.

~~~

Dec. 30—1936   Luray, Va

Mr. J.R. Lassiter

My dear sir: Will you please let me have the house that Velt Nicholson lives in when he moves? The road is so bad to go out and in over. I am on the Relief and if I stay here I would have five miles to bring the food stuff home. I con not get a doctor to come to see me when I am sick where I am at. Please let me have the house. Velt is going to move in about ten days. You know I con not stay here since I have been left alone. If you will let me move in the house it will be a great help to me. As those who con help me con get to me there. I need the house worse than any one else who has been asking you for it. So please let me have it, as I need it so bad. Please let me know at once.

Yours truly,
Mrs. Woodie Corbin,[1]
c/o Haywood Taylor,
Luray, Va.

1. Dora Corbin was the wife of Marvin "Woodie" Corbin, and the couple were tenants in Page County. Woodie Corbin was Teeny Florence Corbin Nicholson's brother.

Defending Honor

During 1937, residents continued to write to park officials to clarify the rules. Often the policies and procedures were confusing to them, as they heard different stories among neighbors and from park rangers and CCC workers. Increasingly, the request for clarification of rules became a statement about the park's responsibility in helping residents resolve their problems or disputes with neighbors. What began in 1936 continued in 1937 and 1938 as residents wrote to park officials to remind them of their obligation in assisting residents who lived on park property. Similarly, requests to collect wood and cultivate crops continued during this time.

As residents lived under special use permits for multiple years and their interactions with park officials increased, they felt compelled to defend their honor when they were accused of breaking park policies. As conveyed in Lillie Herring's letter in 1935, several of these residents resented the ways that they were seen by park and homestead officials, and their letters reveal their increasing frustration with the situation and the assumptions made about them. As is evident in John T. Nicholson's letter of January 29, 1937, he felt compelled to take the windows from his home because of the inevitable vandalism. His letter defends his position and his moral character, explaining his actions to park officials. The residents' letters also increasingly reported neighbors' infractions as they struggled to maintain their lives.

In a different sense, Walter Delan Taylor defends his honor by detailing the ways that he is one of the most qualified in the region to be employed by the park to document and teach about the wildlife and nature in the region. Although a few other letter writers requested work from the park (see Lillie Pearl Nicholson Campbell's letter of August 18, 1937, asking Lassiter to find work for her son through the nearby CCC camp, and Luther Corbin's request of March 3, 1936, for work "looking after the rivers and game"), Taylor requested that he be employed to teach tourists about the wildlife and nature in the park and to photograph the area to document the natural history of the park. Taylor's letter of October 7, 1937, lists in detail his expertise in the area and illustrates his vast knowledge of and interest in preserving its wildlife and nature. In this way, Taylor countered the assumption that outsiders would be the best people to serve as rangers, historians, or naturalists for the park.

Jan 1 1937

Dear Sir
Mr Zerkel

I am going to write you a few lines this morning I would like to move the hay on the place that I moved away from this year I live on Jorning plac and if you can fix for Me to Make the hay I will look after this place all I can and if I sea any thing going wrong I will let you no at wonce abut it and you pleas let me no about this Matter as soon as you can

From Robert Matthews[1]
Bentonville Va

1. See also the letters of December 16, 1935; February 24, 1936; and March 29 and May 26, 1937; and the letter written by Mrs. Robert Matthews dated September 6, 1936.

Jan. 28—1937　　Luray, Va.

Mr R. Taylor Haskins,
Luray, Va.

Dear Chief Ranger, may this please your honor to carefully read and consider every word of this letter.

I humbly beg of your honor to say, that I certainly do regret that I took those windows, but it was like I told you. I did not want to do so, before I seen you or my friend, Mr. J. R. Lassiter, but had waited untill I could see you I would not get them because some other folks came the next day to get them. I needed the windows bad in my house, and that is the only reason why I went and got them. I had no thought as to stealing, I abhor, and shrink from the thought of such a thing small or great in vaule, but I simpley took them because I heard that nothing was to be taken out of the Park, but that we could take from one house and repair another in the Park where there was a house vacated and not reserved as there has been some here in Nicholson Hollow that has been set a side if I have been rightly informed. I did not Know that Buck Dodson needed the windows.

Dear Chief, since I have learned that this displeased you, I have been hurt and troubled over it for more than you may imagine, and I have been on my knees before the Lord Jesus Christ—My Saviour, Judged and confessed to Him and has received pardon and are now happy with Him about it. Listen, "if we confess our sins, he is faithful and just to forgive us our sins and to cleanse us from all unrighteousness" (1 John 1:9)

And now I humbly beg of your honor that you may be pleased to pardon me for displeasing you in taking those windows, and assure me that you feel towards me the same, and will do by me from nown on the same as you would, had this never happened by me.

I say this Mr. Hoskins, because I am a true Christian, and are grived very much over it. And the word says, "Confess your faults one to another, and pray one for another" (James 5:16). This I gladly do when ever I am consciencious of displeasing my Saviour or my fellowman.

Now dear Chief, to prove to you that I am in reality, and are trying hard to lieve as a real Christian should live before God and man, if you say so, I will buy you as many windows as I took from that house and will put them where ever you say. I sincerly mean this because I am grived and hurt very much over it since I saw that you were displeased because I did so, but I hope you will gladly pardon me for doing so, as I humbly assure you that I will be very careful from now on in obeying the rules and regulations of you Park Officials. Indeed I have obeyed the special used permitt to the very letter and have nothing to regret as to this, and shall continue to do so as long as it please you Park officials to permitt me to remain in the Park. I feel very grateful and thankful to you and all the park officials who has had part in granting me the priviledge of remaining in the Park, and especially to the Superintendent of the Park, my beloved and honored friend Mr. J. R. Lassiter,

Dear Chief, if the thing I am writing you about has come to the ears of my friend, Mr. J.R. Lassiter, and he is displeased, please explain it all to him, or let him read this letter that he may fully understand what I did, and why I did it, and how I am now hurt and grived over it, and how I desire to be pardoned by all who has been displease by it, and how I now offer to replace that which I took.

Now dear Chief, in closing this feeble letter, let me congratulate you Park Officials with many heart felts thanks for granting me another year's stay in the Park, I greatly appreciate this more than my vocabulary can express. I am writing a book on the Bible, and hope that I can remain here in my quite home untill I have the manuscript ready for the proof reader.

Please excuse poor writing and all mistakes as I never had the opportunity of going to school as much as one day in all my life so far to learn to read and write. What little education I have, I picked it up here and there.

Affectionatly your obedient friend

John T. Nicholson,[1]

c/o Haywood Taylor,

Luray, Va.

P.S. by this address I get my mail on the Skyline Drive at the Rock Crusher, where I meet the mail on the way to Skyland, Va

1. See also the letters of September 11, 1935, and September 20, 1937, and the letters written by Mrs. John R. Nicholson, John T.'s mother, dated March 5 and May 7, 1936.

<div align="center">~~~~</div>

Feb 5 1937   Syria Virginia

Dear Mr Hoskins

I heard that you are going to move — and —[1] to the Feble mind Colinly if you do Please move me in that house as Mr. Smith that live there is my Brother and that house wold suit me I could get my mail every day and I could my food Broght to me and I wold have some Fruit and I wold Be on the road so a Dr could reach me whare I live it is 3 miles to the nears narber no road up the mountin Just a Path and a Bad way I am 76 years old and if you can Please let me have that house and move me as soon as you take thim a way Please see Mrs Humrickhouse she was to see me some time a go and Said she wold try to get me a Place off of this mountin

your truly Mrs WA Nicholson[2]

1. To protect the privacy of the persons to whom Mrs. Nicholson refers, I have removed their names.

2. Barbara Allen Smith Nicholson was the wife of William Aldridge Nicholson. See also the letters of 1935 (no date; end of the year) and February 15, 1937, and the letter of her son, Kenneth W. Nicholson, dated April 27, 1935.

Nethers Va 1937 Febuary 9

Dear Sir J R lassiter i want to no frome you if the home Steads Be redy this Spring Fore the Madison Peple if not you leat me no at once I got Some Work to do one the Fruit trees this Spring i like to go a head and have Some grainy stuff fore this coming winter you rite and give me Some Jugement a Bout it so i can now what to do

yours truly
Frome Dennis Corbin[1]
nethers Va

1. See also the letters of January 31, 1936, and March 10, 1937.

Feb. 15, 1937   Syria Va

Mr. RT Hoskins
I written you some time a go a bouat the house that the Corbins live in and I have been told that you Said I could get the house But you was going to put Mrs Carrie Nicholson in the house with me that wont suit me for she cant get a long with her ond chirldren and she has sweet hearts and I am old and wont to Be a lone I wold like to have the house But I cant move in with no one I wish you wold come to see me as I wold like to talk with you if you wold let me have the house you wold have to get the CCC Boys to helpe me move in the house and if you let me have the Place Please let me have in time to Put out a Early garden Please try and come to see me as I wold like to talk with you I am your truly

Mrs WA Nicholson[1]

1. Barbara Allen Smith Nicholson. See also the letters of 1935 (no date; end of the year) and February 5 and 15, 1937. Nicholson may be talking about Carrie Weakley Nicholson, the wife of John Nicholson, but that has not been verified.

~~~

Nethers Va   March 10 1937

Dear Mr. lassiter

i rite to you Sealrul Weeks ago and Mr taylor Hoskins did promiss to see me to talk with me a Bout waat i writen to you and i hant seen hime yeat Mr lassiter yo no i did Sine a Special use permit to live at my home untill the home Steades ar redy fore occupancy and yo no the time has come to go to work and to have Somthing to Eat fore this winter i am going now to prune the apples treeas and to ceep the Bushines cut frome around thim this year and to Farme the land i did 1935—i Ben a looking to heare frome yo long a go what i rite to yo look like it Shold wold Be Satisfaction with you yours truly

                                        Mr Dennis Corbin[1]
                                                  nethers Va

ancer soon

i am going to oBay the rules i aint going on no one place to git nothing and no one aint coming on my place to git nothing and that is Fair a man should have what he work fore

1. See also the letters of January 31, 1936, and February 9, 1937.

~~~

Skyland, Va.   March 13, 1937

Mr. R. Taylor Hoskins
My Dear Sir.
I am writing you on business of the way I am treated.

Buck Corbins family just keeps milking my cows and I give them milk every time they come after it. They go down on the grazing farm below them and milk the cows almost every time they find the cows over there. Bucks daughter said that her father said that he was going to farm this year and that he was not going to make any fence around his crop and just as soon as my cows come over there he was going to lock them up in the barn and said that my son as you either would not turn them out until he got pay.

They done my cows bad last year they would milk them and take thire bells off and cut a part of thire tails off and made other threats.

Dont understand me to say that Buck himsef milks them but tells his children to do so. He has some children no one cant trust for any thing.

Mr. Hoskins Please get him moved soon as you can.

But if you leave it to him he wont move at all. He just laughs and says he can go and look at any place and say that it dont suit him and that he can stay where he is now.

Please Mr. Hoskins dont mention this to Buck or any one that would tell him Because if he knew it there is no telling what kind of private in-jure he would do to me, and please have my house fix up as soon as you can for it is in such bad shape.

Remember me to your wife.

Respt. Mrs Bailey Nicholson.[1]

1. Teeny Florence Corbin Nicholson. Buck's wife, Fanney, was Teeny's sister. See also the letters of December 29, 1934, and March 8 and 26, April 13, and August 7, 1938, and the letters written by her son, Richard Nicholson, dated November 11, 1935; August 10, 1936; and August 7, 1945 (the last in the epilogue, on pp. 159–60).

Skyland, Va.   March 23–37

Mr. R. Taylor Hoskins
Dear Sir,
Just a few lines to ask you if I can have some of the Roofing paper on the houes at Skyland that are being tore down as my house roof leakes so bad. One of the men at Skyland told me that I could have it but I dont want to take it with out asking you.
Please let me know soon.

Yous truly,
Noah Nicholson[1]

1. Noah Nicholson was Oscar Nicholson's son (and was Buck Corbin's brother-in-law). See also the letter of November 15, 1937.

March the 24 1937   Stanley Va R1

Mr. JR Lasiter

dear Sir I want to no who gave fread Meadows Permission to tear down
Walker Jenkins building and moove it off of the Park Land Mr Hoskins
told me that no one living out of the Park was not alawed to come in and
take Eny thaing out and them that lived in side was not alawed to take
Eny thaing out & so I want to no whear Meadows gets his a thoritie from

as Ever W.L. Cave[1]

1. Walter Lee Cave was Click Cave's son-in-law and G. A. Cave's nephew.

March 26/37   Stanley va

Mr Zerkle
Luray Va

My Dear Sir   Having Studied over the matter ar i want to do the right
thing by every body and not be contrary iff you will mail me one of your
last permits or tell mr Hoskins to come around i will sign it ar i have all-
ready found out many hard feelings and troubles can be stopped and still
ar i have lived hear all my life and tried to life right and be at feace with
my fellowmen and i want to continue to do so and to cooperate with you
people and still let me say i neal your assistence to try to get me located
elcewhere so iff you can help me any way it will be greatly appreciated

sincerely your friend

G a Cave[1]

1. G. A. "Gird" Cave was the preacher of Dark Hollow Church and was Click
Cave's brother. Gird owned sixteen acres in Dark Hollow and was paid $755 by the
state. After his relocation, Cave was the minister of Inland Mission Church in Page
County. See also the letters of June 5 and 14 and December 1, 1937, and February 5
and 10, April 1, and November 3, 1938.

March 29 1937

Dear Sir

Mr Zerkel

I am going to write you again about the making the Hay on the place where I lived I need the hay so much and now their are about 30 head of cattle pasturing on the plase now and if you all are going to let me make the hay I am going to try to keep the cattle out the man wanted me to let his cattle run up their when I lived their and now he thinks no wone lives their and can pasture all the summer and he has 2 or more farms and he dos not need it like I do for I do not have any akre or any hay to mak and pleas let me here from you as soon as you can and if you have not any thing to do with this matter I am asking you to pleas help me with this matter

yours very truly

Robert Matthews[1]

Bentonville Va

1. See also the letters of December 16, 1935; February 24, 1936; and January 1 and May 26, 1937; and the letter written by Mrs. Robert Matthews, dated September 6, 1936.

april the 13

dear sir just a few lines to you to see if you will get ervin out of jail mr hoskins we need him so bad Click ant aBle to do much work an you all make ant so please Bring him home Sunday we need him more than ever Click dont have work to do when ervin is at home an his wife would Be so glad for you to Bring ervin home the good lord tell us to help to Bear one a nuthers Burdens so you do all you can for ervin mr hoskins i dont think tha treated Click rite tha Bought for others a real good place i think tha arto Bought us a place whire we liked this place is not wuth nuthing But a garden an we ant use to that it dont run lik i am at have own duglas is her yet an ant got us home i think tha arto get him a place to live as same as same tha have got home whire dont need it as Bad as he does he want to make garden you Tell Them to help duglas out a little and try to get him

a place so do all you can for evin an Bring him home at easter we would
love for him to Be her at easter

yours truly
from Mrs Click Cave[1]

1. Lilly Obelia Cave, Click Milam Cave's wife. See also the letter of April 16, 1937.

~~~

<div align="center">April 14, 1937</div>

Mr. R. Taylor Hoskins
I would like for you to let me have the Barn lot for a garden if you would
it is a small Place an no sod on it an if you would I will appreciate very
much an if you let me have it you rite an let me know at once

<div align="right">Yours Truely
Lacy Taylor</div>

address Mr. Lacy Taylor
    Fletcher Va

~~~

april the 16

mr hoskins just a few lines to let you no how much difernce tha make in
helping pople you no tha told me tha was going to get me some house
propert an i never have seen a thing an i no of others tha have got nice
things an the lord no i need things more than some others i no of i surly
would Be glad of some things i dont think it rite to treat some Better than
you do others it seem to us the ones dont need help the ones that gets all
the help i think tha will have to help duglas out he here yet an ant got no
place yet tha want a place to move to so tha can make garden mr hoskins
you please Bring ervins switch key an dresing permit

yours truly
Mrs Click Cave[1]

1. Lilly Obelia Cave, Click Milam Cave's wife. See also the letter of April 13, 1937.

[received Apr 30 1937]

Mr Lassiter
i am writing you this morning to tell you about people pasturing here in
the park as you all have told me to tell you if eny thing went wrong so i
guess you Know ausby Buracker moved off the park on spitler place now.
Edward Jenkins is tearing the lumber aot carring it off and pasturing his
2 cows in here where i live and i have not got fence to turn them so i
would like for you to Send him notice at once to Keep his cows off he tore
the fence down to turn them in yesterday i fixed the place and told him to
keep them so this morning he tore the wire open and turned them Back so
you Bring past notices or mail them to me at once Becuase there is more
people Turns Their cows out on the public Road and they can go where
they please i will Be glad when i can move to the home Steds So they wont
have me to pick on So you send or Bring notices to put up to keep all stock
under fence

Raymond Seal
Stanley Va

to Mr Lassiter
PS
could you all give me work around at the homes soon if so let me know at
once

[stamped received May 26, 1937]

Dear sir
   Mr Laster
   I am writing you a few lines to night again about the hay on the place
in wich I lived I think it is a bad thing to sea it all go to wast as bad as I
need it and as much work as I did on it last year and if you cant tell me
any thing about it would you pleas send me the head managers adress and
I will write to him and sea what he says about is

Very truly yours
Robert Matthews[1]
Bentonville Va

1. See also the letters of December 16, 1935; February 24, 1936; and January 1 and March 29, 1937; and the letter written by Mrs. Robert Matthews dated September 6, 1936.

~~~

Stanly Va   June 5 37[1]

Mr Hoskins Park ranger
    Luray Va
dear Mr Hoskins Since our last conversation i have kept the children off the road but their are some things that i would like verry much to know i am Sure you do not want to be no respect of person their are Some you have prommissed to do some things for iff they would Keep their Children off the road So my wife and myself would like to see you and have a talk iff you will come around we do not want to fuss but just to talk Some things over their are lots of others that are Still Selling but i am not complaining about that for i am Sure They need all they can get So i am wrighting you this personal do not think i am your enemy for i am not i am your friend and want you to be mine yet i have tryed to live honest and make my living honest yet i am here as you know as a man with good understanding i havent bin given a squar deal by the Coart ner [nor] the relief workers yet perhaps you thought i was doing wrong by letting the children go on the road yet iff you Knew some things you would change your mind

So you Come around and lets talk it over i want to be a friend to evey body as Some day we must all Stand before the Judgement to give an account of our lives whether they are good or bad So iff we make it hard on others it will be Terrible for us Some day So this is ritten

as a friend
Sincerly
G a Cave[2]

1. On the same day, Cave also wrote a similar letter to Superintendent Lassiter addressing the same concerns.
2. G. A. "Gird" Cave. See also the letters of March 26, June 14, and December 1, 1937, and February 5 and 10, April 1, and November 3, 1938.

Stanly Va   June 14/37

Mr Taylor Hoskins
dear Mr Hoskins
My dear Sir i am wrighting you the second letter as not hearing any thing
or seeing you Since i ritten to you you knows as i told you that i wanted to
do what was wright and help you people as far as possible So it Seems that
we have bin laid aSide by all i have bin keeping the children off the road
but others are not off So as i understand you told Some parties iff they
would Stay off you would See that they would get Some help So as i told
you in my other letter i dont believe you want to be a respector of persons
and we at present are in need the children have no way to get them any
Clothes and i dont have a chance to work but verry little as i have to work
my craf and the boy is quitting the Camp after this month as he has been
there 2 years and he is tired of the Camp So as i have never bin helped by
the relief but verry little i am going to ask you to See iff we can get Something to furnish the children in Clothes and again i have a very hard job
with pick and shovel and not able to Stand hard work as i once did So i am
wright you this as i dont want to give you people no trouble but iff we
cant make no arrangements the children will have to try and make Something Some way iff it is by Selling flowers but hope they will not have to
So please let me hear from you an come down to the house we would like
to See you

Sincerly
G a Cave[1]

1. See also the letters of March 26, June 5, and December 1, 1937, and February 5
and 10, April 1, and November 3, 1938.

Skyland Va   June 22, 1937

Dear Mr. J. R. Laster.
I am writing you to tell you how the people are going on in Nicholson
Holly. Every Saturday and Sunday they makes whiskey. and the men Sits
on the Road Side. and talk dirty Talk to little children and alsoe keeps it

to sell to mairried men. and you know all the mairried men needs all the money They makes for their Family. and the ones That makes the whiskey is Walter Nicholson and Luther Corbin. and alsoe my own husband goes Down to his brother Luther and Drink with them. and alsoe it the same way down in Oldrag Holly. it nothing kept at charley But a drink Shop. and alsoe Eddie Nicholson and Bennie Sisk and his son do his bring whiskey Their and haul their wifes crying. From your Friend Mrs. Charles Corbin.[1]

1. Fanney Corbin. See also the letter of March 3, 1936.

～～～

Aug the 18th 1937   Nethers Va

Mr. Lassiter

Dear Sir i am riting you a few lines to see if you wont do me the favor to get my boy in the CC camp for me as i am disable to go Around An tind to this an his father wont never look out for mine er the childrens welfare as we are in bad need of things now An got no money to Buy feed for hogs— nor for the family An ever Since the work has bin closed out up at big medows my man hasent worked a day no where home nor a broad for the Hacel People jest Keep on having him to try to Sell all their moon Shine liquor for them at they makes an he doesent do nothing but fool with it for them an cant make enough out of it to Keep Bread for the family so if they aint made to Stop making liquor So at Jim will try to work at something else i jest see at the family is going to nothing for the need of Some help so i hope you will do me this favor at once so he can go rite on in i would rather if you can get him in to put him at no 10. camp if you posible can so he can come home once a month he is 17-years old an hasent none of the family got no job an he wants to get in an i havent no way to go to th office with him to sine him up an his father wont pay no attention to it an i also would bee ever so much oblice to you if you would sind the state officers on the hacel mountain an break up this moon shine buisness as my son lives up there an cecil nicholson was at his house the other nite drunk an fussing A round an tried to knock my boy in the head with a pece of iron. so Please do all you can for me on this work as i am Kept worried so i cant rest none day er nite to do me any good my nerves is jest all to

pecies with the worries them an my husband gives me over this work. an
Jim Lillard wont come up there to look after them for i have told him a
bout them 3 er 4 times an yet he wont do nothing i said when one er 2
gets killed it will bee to late to do any thing then so please do this at once
yours very respect

Mrs Jas Campbell[1]

1. Lillie Pearl Nicholson Campbell. See also the letters of November 6 and 22,
1936; November 30, 1937; and January 8 and February 14, 1938.

Stanley Va   Aug 26

Dear Mr Hoskins I am writing to ask favore of you. This Place where Mr
Fred Seal lives cloce to Park line is a lot of old Builten where Mr Pritz
once raised chickens. I surly would apprciate if you give me enough of that
old lumber to Build me Hog Pen. as Mr seal will take Home stead at Ida
I live close to Park line over on Hill a bove Knights Store Hoping you will
grant me this favor

Cincerly   Mrs. C.T. Taylor[1]
Stanley Va R1

1. Elizabeth Mildred Stoneberger Taylor (Carrie Belle Stonberger Taylor's sister)
was the wife of Charles Thornton Taylor (Page County) and sister-in-law of Robert
Lorenzo Eugene Taylor. See also R. L. Taylor's letters of November 8 and 17, 1937,
and February 14 and 21, 1938.

Sept. 20th, 1937   Nethers, Va.

Mr. J.R. Lassiter, Esq.
Luray, Va.

My dear friend Mr. Lassiter, I hope this may please your honor to carefully read and consider every word of this letter. Not that I mean to persuade you to do any thing that is contrary to your power, but I believe you
will do any thing for us that is within your power.

I have been hearing a strong talk for the last few weeks from different
ones, that all of the people in the Park will have to move out this fall. As to
all this, I keep quite, and tell the folks, "Yes, we may have to move out at

any time." I do not tell them of my hope of being allowed to remain for a while yet any way. I find some is waiting and wanting to go, and others do not care much to go.

But, Mr. Lassiter, if it please your honor to bear with me, I find the thought of having to move out very hurtful to some, and I appeal to you humbly and most kindly, in hope that you will do all you can to permit us to remain here for at least one more winter.

Mr. Lassiter, I know that you are holding a big position, and for that reason you can not afford to say, nor make any promises what you will do for us, and especially in these days when one hardly know who to trust with a secret word or with any thing else. For that reason I am not going to ask you to tell me what you will do, even if it is possible for you to help us out in staying on here for awhile longer, but I will wait and see, because I believe your generous heart will do all it can to permit us to remain on here awhile longer if it is in your power.

May I beg of your honor to say, I know from your pleasant look and your disposition that you are a real man at heart, and no doubt, would be glad for us to remain on here in the Park, may be for years yet, so far as you are concerned. Therefore, I hope you will speak to the higher officials on our behalf, indeed, I believe you will.

Now Mr. Lassiter, look at your friend, George T. Corbin, how sad he looks when he talks about having to move out. I feel sorry for him, his wife and son is sick, and to move out might make them worse.

Now in closing, your honor please, if there is any thing that you can do or say that will help to prolong our stay here, please do so. Indeed, as already said above, I believe you will if you can. You will be blessed by the Lord.

"Blessed is he that considereth the poor, the Lord will deliver him in the time of trouble. The Lord will preserve him, and keep him alive, and he shall be blessed upon the earth, and will not deliver him unto the will of his enemies" (Psa. 41: 1,2).

Very sincerely yours.

John T. Nicholson,[1]

P.S. I expect no reply to this. You understand.

---

1. See also the letters of September 11, 1935, and January 28, 1937, and the letters written by Elizabeth Corbin Nicholson (Mrs. John R. "Russ" Nicholson), John T.'s mother, dated March 5 and May 7, 1936.

Syria Va   Sept the 20th 1937

Mr Hoskin you Please Write to Mr Blandford and tell him to Send my
Boy home I have got a lot of apples and no one to help me pick them you
Please write and tell them to Send him home the first of octoBer to help
me I ant got no help at all you Please Do this for me as I have no one to
help me out yours truly

Walter Meadows
Syria Va

october 7 1937

Dear Mr laseter i want to ask if we will Be alaw to stay here in aur home
an other year if we are and can stay i wold Be glad to no as we have no
ather Place to go and if we can leese ar stay Please let us no as if we do
stay i want to ask if we Can have some of that old lumber at skyland to repair our houses and i want to ask if you will give me some work up here to
take care i will say if you will furnish me with a good camry [camera] and
pay me something i will take Pictures at the forest in all the Park and all
the clifts and falls and bieuty of lots of Placeses that has not as yet Bin
taken as they ane not taken Pictures of ather Placese dont know af hundreds of ather grate Placese and the name of them an i will furnish my
awn Panerid and take the Pictures and you can alow me something for
this work i want to say to all the Park athoritie this is the kinds af what is
in Park i want to give a little illistration of the different kinds of forest
that is in the Shanadoah Natianal Park and all so the different kinds of
Vines and Berryes and weeds and flowers now They is

12 kinds ake	3 kinds ellers	2 hasel Bushes
64 kinds hickry	1 kin cucumber tree	2 kind lacus
4 kinds Pines	1 Paisars dog wood	1 kind chestnut
11 dog wood	1 white walnut	2 kind Payler
11 len wood or Butter	1 Beach walnut	1 red Bud
2 kinds wild cherry	1 serlen Bark	2 Black Berrye
2 kinds Burch	1 Sasafras	2 rasberyes

2 huckle Berrys	48 kinds flours and	6 kinds rings vines
2 goos Bereys	weeds	1 wild cut leaf
2 curut Bushes		

now if you will Call a meeting i will Come to it and explain how all this grow and how it Producese it fruits now we have 20 Kinds small Birds

1 kind Pheasfant	1 kind water	4 kinds small flyes
1 kind Patridges	2 kind fish	1 silver Payler
1 kind snipe	1 kind eal	1 lilack
1 craw	1 taripen	1 PaPo tree
1 ravin	1 turtle	1 Banagllis tree
1 Ponddywid	3 kind frogs	1 iran waud
2 kinds hawk	3 kind ants	4 kinds Beese
12 kinds fur Paring	5 kind Bugs	2 kind rats
animals	8 kind gnats	3 kind lizards
7 kind snakes	1 kind machetes	1 water skypes
3 kinds are	5 kind Buttes fly	

af the forest game and fish and flaurs as i will Be rite here nite and day to Protect all thes and i will take a Pride in taking Care af all the People that Came in to the Park Please do what you Can for us in all this i hope you and all your People and family are enjoing the Best of helth yours verry truly WD Taylor[1]

skyland Va

PS Please let me no as you can to all this and i hope you may give me a job at something ar help me to get a Job as if you and the ather athorities of the Park give me a job i will do all i Can in Protecting every thing and Shaw all the People that came in here first what is in the Park and Can Shaw them all they most Bieuty at this Park an for ever Be an the look out for every thing that may happen in the Park let me no if you will help us to fix my aur house for the winte ar let us fix it up

1. Walter Delan Taylor. This letter is unique in the archives. Taylor makes a case for the park to hire him as an expert on the land and animals in the area. See also the letters of December 21, 1935; February 19 and March 16, 1936; October 24, 1937; and January 24, 1938.

actober 24, 1937   from WD Taylor[1]

Dear Mr Hoskins i want to say that we wanted to move aut this fall But
the hause that we were to move two had no water an it at all nor nane
claser than 3 hundreds yards away an Same ather mans land and to get
water to water aur cow would Be half mile away no seller at all and no
Barn and a grate und can rite against the corner of the kitchen and i saw
mrs humrick house and she sed it were not Paid for so you see they were
not no chance moveing there at all saw the Cline house Place at the foot
at the mauntain an the old Skyland road is for sale and Can Be Baught for
$450 four hundred and fifty dollars and can give a deed for it same day
it is Baught and We Can move rite aut next day i hape you may see mrs
humrick house and get her to get this for us as they want to sell it at ance
if they get this Place in 10 days we Can get aut if they dont get us a home
aur house will have to Be repaird as we Cant stay in it this way and you
can Haul us that lumber at Berry Bernies old Place to fix it i want to ask
if we Can have the wire around aur yards and fence to fix a fience if we
move aut

1. See also the letters of December 21, 1935; February 19 and March 16, 1936;
October 7, 1937; and January 24, 1938.

Oct. 25. 1937   Mr. Lasader Dear sir

Mr. j N Weakly told me to call your attention for a load of wood that he
was shure you had forgot that was my mother down to see you if there
would be such as for me to get wood i am a widow with four small Kids
of Elbert C Gray deceased ilive Just below Mr E. D. Weakleys store pine
grove ihate to be so much trouble to people but that is the only way for me
Just come and see my condition yours truly

Mrs. Elbert C Gray[1]

1. Mary Elizabeth Jenkins Gray. She and her husband lived in the home of her father, Robert L. Jenkins. Jenkins owned fifty-two acres on tract 406 in Page County,
land that was originally surveyed but not purchased for the park.

~~~

[received] Nov 5 1937

R Taler hoskins
Depart ment of the interior
Luray Va
mr hoskins I would Be very thankful to you if you would let me and Irie
Brown the lumber in the house Cary Nicholson lives in to fix our houses
we will tair it down and move it away if Please Right and let me no if I can
get it we will Clean it up nice

<div style="text-align: right">

Plase let me By Return Mail
from your friend
Charles E. Dyer[1]
Syria Va

</div>

1. See also the letters of April 8 and 10, 1936, and March 14 and August 12, 1938,
and the letter of Charles's wife, Lizzie Nicholson Dyer, dated May 8, 1936.

~~~

Stanley Va   R1 Box 31   Nov. 8, 1937

Mr. Taylor Hoskins
Chief Ranger
S.N.P.
Luray Va
Dear sir: Will you come up by Knight's Store Tues. morning or come
down this way Tues. eve. and stop at My place? The first house coming
down, in the turn I wish to see you on business Sometime ago a G. I. pick
up truck ran in to my Stable and knocked it down the Driver left as soon
as he could get away before I could get out there. The crash and pulling it
out of the road about destroyed the lumber and now I must have a Stable
to store my feed in. I can't buy any lumber here and as the old buildings
where Fred Seal lived are to be torn down and will not be of any use to
the Gov. or any damage either I am asking you to allow me to get these
old buildings to build me another Stable. As the Gov. truck tore mine
down. I am not asking you to give or sell me these buildings, but allow me
to get them to replace the damage done me to replace mine. I think this

will be the best way to settle this matter The man who did this is Still in the [CCC] Camp.

Don't you think it would be fair to replace my stable or repay me by letting me get these old buildings? I think as I am willing to accept these old buildings in lieu of a Money settlement It would be the Just thing to do to let me get these buildings and end the matter If you can't come up or down Tues. Write me by return mail as some of the lumber is disappearing

Respt yours
R.L. Taylor[1]

P.S. inquire at Knight's Store for me.   R.

1. Robert Lorenzo Eugene Taylor, listed as a public school teacher in Page County in the 1930 census, was married to Carrie Belle Stoneberger and was the brother of Charles Thornton Taylor. Robert Taylor owned 174 acres on tract 18 in Greene County and was paid $2,362 by the state. Ranger Hoskins's return letter says, "I have discussed this matter with Superintendent Lassiter, and he informed me that he had no authority to give you the buildings requested." See Taylor's reply of November 17, 1937, and two other letters, dated February 14 and 21, 1938.

Skyland. Va.   Nove 15, 1937

Mr Taylor Hoskins
Luray Va.
Dear Sir, Just a few lines concerning moving. I will ask you to give me till the last of this month ar the frist of next month, as I have not had time to work the road and when it is worked it will have to lay for a few days to settle before a truck could get over it and I also have a lot of wood cut for Skyland that I would like to get hauled at once, and please notify me at least 3 ar 4 days before you send the trucks to move. I also need the money for the wood to get my children cloths. Please ancr soon. Hopng you can do me this favor and ablige

Yours truly,
Oscar Nicholson.[1]

1. Oscar O. Nicholson was George Bailey Nicholson's brother and was married to Ida F. Corbin Nicholson. Oscar Nicholson owned seven acres on tract 101 in Madison County and was paid $510 by the state. Ida Nicholson owned fifty-two acres on tract 252 in Rappahannock County and was paid $550 by the state.

Madison County resident Oscar
Nicholson, who lost his home.
(Library of Congress, Prints &
Photographs Division, FSA-
OWI Collection, reproduction
number LC-USF33-T01-002185
DLC; photograph by C. Arthur
Rothstein, 1935; used by
permission of Nicholson's family
and Grace Rothstein)

Stanley Va   Nov. 17, 1937

Mr. J. R. Lassiter
Luray, Va.
Dear sir:

   In reference to what you say on the opposite side of this sheet. I am not
asking you to give me anything or sell me anything. I am only asking you
to replace Damages done me by some one in your dept. and I believe under your jurisdiction. Anyway a G.I. truck did me the damage. I know you
do not have the authority to give or sell me these buildings but I believe
you have the authority to replace the damage done by a G. I. employee All
I ask is that you allow me to go get enough old lumber to replace damage

done me. When it is worth nothing to the Gov. and is being taken away by others. Now Mr. Lassiter if I go and get enough lumber to pay for damages, What will you say or do about it? Remember the G. I. men and with a G. I truck did the damages and did not stop after hitting the Stable. Let me hear from you by return mail. If answer is not satisfactorily, I will take the matter up with the Dept at Washington. You had better let me get the lumber and it will close the matter and no one hurt.

Respt

R.L. Taylor[1]

1. Robert Lorenzo Eugene Taylor. See also the letters of November 8, 1937, and February 14 and 21, 1938.

Nov. 20. 1937   Brightwood Va—

Mr L.F. Zerkel.
Dear friend i am riting you to no if you will give me the lumber that is in the House where Luther Corbin live at when he moves out i would be glad of it i live there a bout 12 months a go so let no by return mail

Yours truly-

W.B. Nicholson-[1]

1. William B. "Buddy" Nicholson was married to Victoria Nicholson, brother of Lillie Pearl Nicholson Campbell. Buddy Nicholson owned twenty-one acres on tract 24 in Madison County and was paid $976 by the state. See also the letter of October 26, 1936.

Nov. 22—1937   Nethers, Va.

Mr. J.R. Lassiter
Luray, Va.
My dear Sir:
Just a few lines to kindly ask you to give me the lumber out of the house Mr. Haywood Nicholson moved from. It belonged to Mrs. Ackie Hudson, before the Park took it over.

I would greatly appreciate your kindness if you would do this for me.

I need some lumber. I sold my home to the Park, and moved out. I am in about three quarters of a mile of this place. Please let me know at once. I am not taking any thing from the houses that has been vacated, and will not unless you give me permission. If you will give me what I need of it, I will clean up and burn up the wast when it is no danger in fire.

Affectionately yours,
V. E. Nicholson,

Dear Mr. Lassiter, if you possible can do so, please let uncle Ease have this house, he needs it to do some repair work. Your friend as ever. John T. Nicholson[1]

1. At the end of Van East Nicholson's letter is a note signed by his nephew, John T. The handwriting of both portions of the letter is very similar and is also similar to the handwriting in John T.'s other handwritten letters, which suggests that he wrote this letter for his uncle. See John T.'s other letters of September 11, 1935, and January 28 and September 20, 1937. Van East Nicholson owned 110 acres on tract 8 in Madison County and was paid $1,532 by the state.

<div align="center">~~~~</div>

Jeffersonton, Va   [received] November 23, 1937

Dear Sir [addressed to Vinson Roads]. I am asking you for some winter apples if it is so you can let me have them I bought a little plase with out eny fruit at all on it They sernldy would be aprecieded if you can let me have them please let me know wether I can get them or not If I can get them tell me where I can get them at the place I lived or some plase else Mr Ambrose Bailey[1]

1. Ambrose Bailey lived in Culpeper County when he wrote this letter, but he had lived in Rappahannock County. He owned 214.5 acres on tract 101 and was paid $1,891 by the state. His property was surveyed as having twenty-seven apple trees.

<div align="center">~~~~</div>

Syria, Va.   Nov. 30, 1937

Dear Mr. Hoskins

We would rather move in Cameron Richards house if you can arrange it so we can move there. but if you can not arrange it we will move in Wade Sisk's house. but Wade Sisk's house is to far up suit us. and that is

Life-tenure residents
George W. and Lucy
E. Hurt, Madison
County. (Courtesy of
the Shenandoah
National Park
Archives; used by
permission of
Nellie F. Seale)

why Camerons house suits us better. but the house needs some work done
on it. so please let us hear from you at once.

Sincerely yours,

Mr. George Hurt[1]

1. George Hurt owned sixteen acres on tract 168 in Madison County and was
paid $420 by the state. George and his wife, Lucy Ellen Sisk Hurt, were granted "life
tenure" so that they could live out their lives in the park. Like John Russ Nicholson,
Matilda Breeden, and about forty other aging residents, the Hurts were granted this
status so that they could remain in the park rather than have to move so late in their
lives. Hurt's letter is written in response to a letter written by Ranger Taylor
Hoskins that suggests that they move to the Wade Sisk home. Hoskins says in his
letter, "If you decide to move, I suggest you do not delay because there is a chance

that some one may steal lumber from the house." The Hurts, however, preferred to move to Cameron Richard's house because of its location.

~~~

Nethers Va   Nov 30/37

Luray Va
Mr. Lassiter Park Supt.
Dear Sir
I have letter from the welfare workers at Elkton Va stateing I could not get home stead as I need one Thousand Dollars for my place I am oweing a few hundred dollars and I want have nothing like that amt after I pay my debts I would like to get a home stead and hope to hear from you why I cant as I am sure you will give me the propper information

resp
James R. Campbell[1]

1. Like the Campbells, many families were promised homesteads if they sold their land to the park. After they sold their land, however, they were assessed by the Resettlement Administration and often did not "qualify" for the government loan needed in order to purchase the homestead. This kind of bureaucracy frustrated many residents because they felt they were not given adequate information. The following letter from Gird Cave reflects a similar frustration. See also the Campbells' letters of November 6 and 22, 1936; August 18, 1937; and January 8 and February 14, 1938.

~~~

Stanley Va   December 1/37

Mr J R Lasiter
Luray Va
dear Mr Lasiter the welfare woman was just hear and Says they Cant buy us a place but wants us to go and rent for our Selves but you Know as for our Contract that i had Signed up for a homestead at ada and now have bin turned down and was turned over to the welfare and they Say we have to rent for our selves So you know that this is not fair as their is people lots younger than i that they have bought homes for and we have had no work for a good while and we dont feel able to go out to rent So we are

ready at any time now to move iff they will furnish us a place as they did
the others So i am willing to do any thing that is any ways right but i cant
See that this deal is any ways right So i am not willing to except it So im
willing to do unto others as i would have them do unto me but i would not
want any body to except a proposition like this So use your influence for
us iff you please as we would like to get moved or Setteled Soon as we
Could as you Know how it would be to be always on a dread not Knowing
what to do So our Old house is gitten a verry bad roof that leaks So we
will have to Soon move or Cover the house So may God Bless you and
yours

Sincerely

G a Cave[1]

1. See also the letters of March 26, June 5, and June 14, 1937, and February 5 and
10, April 1, and November 3, 1938.

RANDOLPH-MACON ACADEMY

Box 641   Front Royal, Va.   Dec. 7, 1937

The Superintendant
The Shenandoah National Park, Luray, Va.
Dear Sir:

I am writing you in behalf of Mr. H. Edgar Merchant, Front Royal, Va.

Last spring, after he had been notified that he must vacate the house
where he is living, he and I began to look for a home for him and his family, consisting of himself, his wife, and an old father who is nearly blind.

We could find two houses for sale: none for rent. The people who
would sell would give possession when they could find a house to move
to. After my duties began here Sept. 15th, I was no longer able to help
him, but he continued to hunt for a place.

Mr. Merchant moved to that place to work for me before 1914, and he
has lived there as a good worker, a good tenant, and a good citizen. As you
possibly know I turned the property over to the State of Va. in Feb. 1935
or '36.

I shall be indebted if the one in charge will take tese facts into consideration, and permit him to remain temporarily.. He will continue his hunt

during the winter, and next June, when my duties here become less insistent, I will join again in seeking a house for him, unless he has found it prior to that time.

Thanking you, in advance, for any consideration you will give this matter, and for your assistance in temporarily providing him a home, I am

Yours very truly,
Chas. L. Melton.[1]

1. See also the letter of September 17, 1934.

[no date but probably 1937 or 1938]

Mr. Freeland. Dear Sir Just a line to let hear that the old mill top is caving in till is geting in a dangerous Shape and the Kitchen it geting in a awful Shape also the House leaks so Bad when it rains it runing my furniture so please try and come down an send some one to look at things. We have Roofing if you could give us some lumber & Frunish the Labor.
I am yours.

Mrs. George Shifflett[1]
Stanardsville, Va
Old Lam Mill

1. According to Lambert's *Undying Past of Shenandoah National Park* (255), George Shifflett was granted a special permit to remain in the park as the caretaker of the Lam Mill.

Maintaining Daily Life

During 1938, as the last of the remaining residents were moved from the park (except those who were given life tenure), letters to park officials continued to be written about harvesting crops, obtaining financial and other assistance from the government, and pointing out the park's responsibility in helping the residents in their tenuous situations. In addition to a steady stream of letters containing similar requests as in previous years, the letters arriving in 1938 reflect an attempt to maintain daily life until the residents were compelled to move. Residents requested loads of wood, apples, small buildings to cover their equipment or salt their meat, and assistance with their bills. While the park was in the process of removing buildings, they were also responsible for the families remaining in the park. In these letters, it is clear that the residents were striving to manage their daily existence despite the fact that their relocation was imminent. Many of the writers during 1938 had written to the headquarters in Luray before, and their familiarity with the rangers and the superintendent is clear.

Mrs. Robert (Rubie C.) Matthews's disappointment in leaving her home (letter of September 6, 1936) and John T. Nicholson's pleas for his neighbor George Corbin (who was also the father-in-law of John T.'s sister, Polly Nicholson Corbin; letter of October 7, 1937) show that many residents loved their homes in the mountains and were deeply saddened to leave them. A few people remained in the park with life-tenure permits (see Lambert's *Undying Past of Shenandoah National Park* for more detail about those granted life tenure), but by the end of 1938, most of the residents had moved permanently from the park and had begun their lives elsewhere, whether they wanted to or not.

~~~

Jan the 8th   Nethers, VA

Mr. J R Lassiter

Dear Sir i am riting you a few lines this morn to let you Know i have
found me a Place—but i cant get prossesions—of it under a month er
more—an Mr- Lassiter i am not—able to pay—all down so i have Pd—out
what i had An i think it would bee nothing but rite for the welfare to pay
the rest on this Place for me. As i have never had any help from them like
they has helped other people i sold my land to the Park at their on [own]
Price an—i feel at they ought to help me out on geting me a home where
i would like to have as its no big place but i feel like if i ever get it Pd
for i could live on it so i hope you can advise me what to do for the best i
would like for you to rite to Miss. humbly house [Humrickhouse] for me
an see at she helps me out on geting my home pd for as i am not able to
work much any more an my wife is in bad health all the time an last fall
i bruised my hand working on the job at big meadows an i wer not able to
work for 2 months an i had to see the Dr. ever ather day. that is why my
store counts an DR bills piled up on me like this an i am short of Paying
out on my home so i hope you can bee of some help to me as i have worked
on Relief work for over 3 years an i never has had no help for my family. er
my stock no help in no way out side of my monthly payments for my work
so i have moved down off the mount—here to JR-Nicholsons place so i feel
at i aught to bee left here untill the man i bought from can find him a place
to go to so you let me hear from you at once an you see miss Humbly
House for me an tell her all about this an tell her i need feed for my cow an
horse an my hogs as i havent had no work now for 2 months an it puts me
in bad shape so i hope to get an order to the store rite a way so i can get
my cow an horse some feed as i am clear out of corn an feed i would bee
glad to bee working on this—iv Pa[1] work now—but i havent got no way
to get to this work so Please let me hear from you at once an you tell Mr
HosKins to let me stay on here untill the other man can find him a place.
as i dont care to move in on him as the house is small—an we coulden
make out for room so i hope to hear from you at once Yours truly J.R
Campbell[2]

1. Campbell is referring to the Works Progress Administration.

2. The handwriting in this letter is similar to that in several of the other letters signed by Lillie Pearl Nicholson Campbell. See also the letters of November 6 and 22, 1936; August 18 and November 30, 1937; and February 14, 1938.

Luray Virginia   Jan. 10th, 1938

Miss Mozelle Cowden
Elkton Va
Dear Miss Cowden

When Russell Broyles had his check Saturday he went for moonshine and got drunk and come home drunk and brought other drunk men there and cussed his mother and me and told us it was his place and we would have to get out.

This is doings that old people like us cant stand and we need the help of the Government right away to see we have decent treatment and a home. Please do it for us old people that cant get along without such help.

Yours
James Buracker[1]

1. James R. Buracher. See also the letter of February 27, 1935. Mozelle Cowden was a social worker who helped several families as they negotiated their lives after the park's establishment. Like many of the advocates in the community, Cowden fowarded this letter to park officials for their assistance.

10 Jan 1938.   Syria Va.

Dear Mr. Hoskiens

Will you Pleas let me Know right at once when I can go to look at that place at Elkton if I am going to Take a Place I got to go at once to prepear for a crop

Yours very Truly
Wes Hurt.

PS. let me Know at once.
    thank you

~~~~~

Jan 21 1938   R #1 Box 185   Elkton, Va.

Dear Madam!

Just a few lines in regard to a plan I have in Mind. I understand the
Park People are moving Charlie Bailey out this week. But I dont guess
they will on account of the rain. I was thinking if you would see Mr.
Zirkle and tell him the circumstances maby he would give me the lumber
in the house to finish mine. I havn't got enough lumber and if I could get
that I could finish my house right away. It is close and I could get it soon
as they moved out. Please see what you can do about it for me. I am off
from work until the 27th and could do a lot of work toward building in
that time.

Thanking you I remain

Yours Truly

Seibert Lam.[1]

1. Seibert Maylon Lam's letter was written to Mable Humrickhouse, the super-
visor of the Department of Public Welfare in Elkton, Rockingham County. The archives contain several letters of correspondence between residents and
Humrickhouse, and between Lassiter and Humrickhouse, as the Department of Public Welfare worked closely with the park administration in assisting some of the residents as they moved out of the park.

~~~~~

Jan. 23 1938

Mr. J R. Lassiter.

Dear Sir—

Just ric [received] a letter from the office asking when I could move. and
to advise the office what I was planing to do I am planning to move as
Soon as Possible. I am going Monday or tuesday to look for a house.

Yours truly

Ralph Cave[1]

1. Ralph Cave was Gird Cave's son. He was one of the many people interviewed
by Dorothy Noble Smith. These oral histories, collected in the late 1970s and early
1980s, are archived at James Madison University's Special Collections in Harrisonburg, Virginia. See the page about the collection on the library's website, http://

www.lib.jmu.edu/special/manuscripts/SNP.aspx. See also D. Smith's *Recollections* and the letters of March 26, June 5 and 14, and December 1, 1937, and February 5 and 10, April 1, and November 3, 1938.

January 24 1938

Dear Mr Haskins

i want to ask that you Please Came aut and tell me what to do in regard to that stable and fience as i would like to Be getting it dawn and ane af those stables will make hadge all he wants the lare stable as the smallest and anely the sides is, sheet arn and all the ruffes ane is sheet arn 45 + 36 in size so you see he Can get all he will want So Came an up and rite me so i will no Just what to do i hape you and wife are well

Cincncerly

W.D Taylor[1]

luray Va.

excuse this Bad Paper and Bad riting

1. Walter Delan Taylor. See also the letters of December 21, 1935; February 19 and March 16, 1936; and October 7 and 24, 1937.

Stanley Va   Feb 5 38

Mr Taylor Hoskins

My dear Sir you please See mr Lasiter and ask him iff i Could get the windows out of the house and iff he Could give me the Church building i would have it moved out of the park and rebuilt again So please let me know at once Send the trucks in tuesday iff the weather is not too bad Ga Cave[1]

1. G. A. "Gird" Cave was the preacher of Dark Hollow Church and in this letter requests materials from that building. The trucks to which he refers were those used by the Civilian Conservation Corps to assist families in moving from the park. See also the letters of March 26, June 5 and 14, and December 1, 1937, and February 10, April 1, and November 3, 1938.

~~~

feb 7 1938

Dear Mr Laster
i am writing you a few lines to ask you if you would give me the house if
i move it i have cash money in the buiden i bought lumber and rebard the
house and barn and bought windows and i have not never resived no helP
at all since i have been here so i Thank you ought to let me have the building all the rest of the familys got thers
    so i hope you will study over it and say yes

                                        from Ben Meadows[1]
                                            yours Truley

    1. See also the letter of April 7, 1936.

~~~

[February 10, 1938]   Shenandoah Va   Rout 1

Mr J R Lasiter
My dear Sir would you please give me the church building and i will have
it moved and the Lumber out of the old house and I would Thank you So
much So I could build a nother little place of worship So let me Know at
once Sincerely Ga Cave[1]

    1. See also the letters of March 26, June 5 and 14, and December 1, 1937, and Feb-
ruary 5, April 1, and November 3, 1938.

~~~

Stanley Va   Feb. 14, 1938

Mr. Hoskins (Chief Ranger)
Luray Va:
Dear sir:
    I got lumber and logs to build Stable not quite enough of either but to-
gether may come out O.K. Many thanks.
    The reason I am Writing you is Every thing that was there is gone and
you will find most of it at or near Frank Taylors He hauled & carried day
and night he and others and I hear it will be divided later. Most of the logs

and lumber is just around a little hill across the creek, up the branch, and up to his place all the best lumber is up at his house I understand all that will not do for building will be sold for wood. I am writing you this to let you Know I did not take advantage of anyone connected with the Park Service

Respt. yours
R.L. Taylor[1]

P.S. Frank Taylor is not the only one who helped themselves
R.

1. Robert Lorenzo Eugene Taylor. See also the letters of November 8 and 17, 1937, and February 21, 1938.

~~~

Feb the 14th 1938   Nethers Va

Mr. J R Lassiter

Dear Sir i am riting you a few lines this morn to let you Know at i wanted to move this wK but now long as things are like it is i dont Know when i can move for i am not able to do nothing my self—an the only Boy i had here to help me out with my work—is gone an if the court dosent free him an sind him on back to me i cant Keep house for i am not able to hire no one an he wer the only boy i have at can cook an help me out with my work an i had left him at home to Keep house for me while i had gone to the hospital —an while i an my Husband wer a way. Mr. Hoskins an Herman come an got him an Albert Nichols Boy an carried them to Harison burg—Jest for throwing An old chimney at wer almost ready to fall it self to an old house. An i feel at if this house was Reserved at Mr Herman & Hoskins Should of notified People a bout it an Put the Sine on it bee fore Dee Corbin moved now he has bin out of it over 2. months an diferent onesses had up set the house rite bad. An i under stood Mr Herman to tell me i could get some of the lumber over there to make Boxes with an so after all this hapen it was marked up govment Prop i dont feel at this is a bit fair to treat no'one a bout their children when its not one-man out of a hundred but what hasent broke the Rules in the Park Area ever Since the gov ment has excepted this land an Mr Herman Knows at i told him a bout Some of them at wer get-ing wood an hauling out building stones out of the Park area bout the

same time at those 2 Boys tore down this old chimney so i feel at if they
can look over old men an Rich men they sertain could look over boys. an
poor boys at that for we hasent got no money to spind out on our Boy—an
i dont feel at Albert has any to put out for his for we Pd—out what litle we
had on us a litle home an yet hasent near got it—Pd—for an Jim er none of
the Boys hasent no work to make nothing not much as 25 cts per day. An if
our boy has to bee took A way from us how can we farm to make any thing
to live on—so i hope at you will see those officers for me—Mr Lassiter an
tell them to see at my boy is forgive This Time for being in co with this
other boy—An i feel sure at he wont ever give the Park People no more
trouble for this is his first time in Any trouble an that is why he left home
as it scared him so he says he coulden stand to go to court for he haden
done nothing he says he diden want Adam to Bother the old Chimney an
he gest done it for fun as he thought i am awful sorry at my boy was along
with him of course this Nichols boy is not no real bad boy—but he is gest
dumb dont realice the danger of things he does so i hope you will rite to
the judge at Harrison burg for me an get him to forgive my son of this as
me an his father hates it so bad for him an he is bout the best one of my
children of course we have tried hard to raise them all rite but you Know it
aint but very few men but what dont do things some times they ought not
well as boys do so i hope you will do all you can for me as i am troubled so
much about this i sure will appreciate you for it an never will for get you
for your Kindness for doing this favor for me

> i beg to remain
> yours very Respect
> Mr & Mrs Jas Campbell[1]

PS—

    Also Mr Lassiter i cant understand why at we coulden get a homestead
for we Sined up for one 4 years ago an think we sold them land an wanted
a gov ment home an we coulden get it er no welfare home either. i cant see
why they make such a big diference on people for my husband has bin on
this relief work ever since it started an we never has got no help in no way
only gest his work at 21 D per month an yet he hasent had no work now
since last July he wants you to see a bout this for him as we need work bad

1. James R. and Lillie Pearl Nicholson Campbell. The letters that are signed
"James R. Campbell" or "Jas R Campbell" are written in the same handwriting as

those signed "Mrs. Jas R Campbell." See also the letters of November 6 and 22, 1936; August 18 and November 30, 1937; and January 8, 1938.

~~~

Stanley Va   Feb. 21, 1938

Mr. J. R. Lassiter
Supt. S.N.P.
Luray Va
Dear sir:

Sometime ago it was agreed that the damage done me by Some one in the Park Service would be settled by restoring damages by bringing me lumber but as it was not convinient to bring it to me. I was told to go get the lumber which I did or had it done as I could not be there. I hired my Bro. C.T. Taylor and Marvin Cave to get this lumber for me and as I expected the Park service to replace damage done by putting the lumber back at my place. Which would have cost the Gov. for tearing this lumber down and delivering it to me and they (the Park Service) failed to do so and there by not being put to this cost. it was just and right for me to get lumber enough to pay damages. This lumber was hauled to my place and I let My Bro. and Mr. Cave have enough of this lumber to pay them for their work. I considered this lumber mine and I could build a stable or sell it. (Am I right?) so I sold that much My Bro. & Mr Cave are order to return this lumber back to the place where it came from. this was my lumber and I am asking you to allow My Bro. & Mr Cave the privilege to Keep what they got from me and they certainly would not be under obligations to return it anywhere but to my place. as it was mine. My damage was 5 times the amt. of lumber I got and I must yet put the stable up and pay for roofing.

Let me hear from you by return mail.

This was not government property after it was brought to me I believe legally & morrally They have a right to the lumber

I hope you will see this as we do.

Respt yours
R.L. Taylor[1]

1. Robert Lorenzo Eugene Taylor. See also the letters of November 8 and 17, 1937, and February 14, 1938.

~~~

Feb 28 1938   Stanley Corbin[1]   Reva Va

Mr JR lassiter dear Mr lassiter i am asking you to do me a favor. Now i
want you to give me the wire around George T Corbin garden whear he
left. he is my father i am a pore man and Need the wire to go around my
garden it ant doing No one No good whear it is at i moved out of the park
and caused you all No truble So plese give it to me as i would bee thankful
for it so plese let me hear from you at once

yours truly

1. See also the letters of February 3, March 2, July 13, and November 28, 1936.

~~~

Syria Va.   March 1, 1938.

Dear Mr Hoskins.

I Would like to move down off the mountain. I Would like to know
what you are going to do with Cameron Richard are you going to make
him move or not I Would like to move down there so I can make my garden but They are burning all the fence from around the garden. and I
would like to set me some hens and raise me some chickens. I sure am getting tired staying on the mountain cameron goes down in orange and
then he comes back and stays in the bed drunk for 3 or 4 days.

Sincerely Yours
Mrs George Hurt.[1]

1. Lucy Ellen Sisk Hurt. The Hurts were granted life tenure by the Park Service.
See also George Hurt's letter of November 30, 1937.

~~~

Flint Hill Va   March 4, 1938

Dear Mr Lassiter

will you please let me move that little meat house from the place I lived
on, Albert Clark place it is the little building where Dudly pullen lived at
the spring house I want it to store some of my thing in which is out in the
weather Mr Dick from no 10 Camp said he would move it any time if you

said so so please drop me a line and let me know at once before it is burnt up or torn down. from

Rasby Clarke.

I live in the home stead at Flint Hill

Skyland. Va.   March 8, 1938

Mr R. Taylor Hoskins
Luray. Va.

My Dear Friend I want you to please haul 2 or 3 loads of wood houled over at my place. a freind looked it over a day or so ago and there is only about a cord of green wood and no one cant cook with green wood. I don't see why this would not be cheaper instead of buying wood over there and geting a truck to haul it. let me know at once the load where you told Richard I could have is all ready. and the lumber at the school house is all ready and could be houled any day Richard or Johny would go with the truck if needed. And Please let me know whot day I will move as I have been sick for the past two weeks and would like to know ahead of time as long as possibel. Johnny will get the lumber from the house I am now living in Just as soon as we move. Please let me hear from you soon so I will know more about what to do. Remember me to your wife. I trust you and yours are well and enjoying the best of health.
Write soon

Resptfully yours
Mrs. Teeny F. Nicholson.[1]

1. See also the letters of December 29, 1934, and March 26, April 13, and August 7, 1938.

March 14, 1938.   Syria V̲a̲

Mr R. Taylor Hoskins
Luray V̲a̲
Dear Sir. As you Know I purchased land which joins the park land. And there is no fence at All between my land and the park land and I am not

financially able to buy the wire to make the line fence would you give me permission to get some Barbed wire which is in the park. as I underStand that there is lots of it in the park especially on the Howard J. Berry Place near Oldrag.[1] So I am hoping you will let me have some wire to make the line fence. as it is needed to keep my cattle off the park land. as I understand Cattle is not permitted to Roam in the park.[2] So please let me hear from you at once

Very truly yours
Charles E. Dyer[3]

1. Like many residents, Dyer refers to specific property by a person's name, giving special significance to the property within the boundaries of the park. The property may have been seen by others as mere land and materials, but the residents saw the property as people's homes.
2. Cattle had previously been allowed to roam in the park.
3. See also the letters of April 8 and 10, 1936; November 5, 1937; and August 12, 1938; and the letter of Charles's wife, Lizzie Nicholson Dyer, dated May 8, 1936.

<div align="center">~~~~~</div>

Skyland. Va   March 26, 38

Mr. R. Taylor Hoskins
My Dear Sir.

Mr Foster was out to see me yeasterday Morning and told us that we could move tuesday and wednesiday I wont go Till Wednesday when the last load of my property is loaded on. Richard told me that you said you Probley would be buisy so if that is the case you cant take me over. if you cant take me please see Mr Fox and see if he wont take me. I have never put any of You all to any troubl to houl me and I think I ought to be taken over to my home any way there is some peopl that has been houled around for about 2 Years and I have never even put the welfare or park Service to any troubl to houl me any where. Also Bucks and Noahs wife was taken in a car. Mr Foster said chase the cows down to Nethers I have a cow that is very bad to chase and I had rather them be loaded on at the housee. Thanking you for your kindness in the past I am

Respt.
Mrs Teeny F. Nicholson[1]

1. See also the letters of December 29, 1934, and March 8, April 13, and August 7, 1938.

Shenandoah Va   April 1 / 1938

Mr Taylor Hoskins

dear mr Hoskins i am Just writing you a few lines concerning the trouble
that Ralph gotten into i dont Know what they did and i am not trying to
uphold them for doing wrong but as you Know they compelled him to
leave the mountains with out giving or wrenting any place at all and
i want you to Consider yourself having a wife and 4 children without any
Job or any thing to go upon and now you all have driven him a way from
home and left his family hear on me to Take Care of and as you Know i
havent had any work for So long and i am not able to take Care of my own
So Just Think for a little as you Treat others That you must Stand Some
day before the Judgement to give an account for your Self So i would love
for you to see the officials to See that his wife and children be given Something to eat as they are in bad need So i am Just writing this to you as a
friend not trying to uphold no one for doing wrong but Just think of little
children going hungry for Something to eat So you please do what you
Can and Consider that none of us have bin good but that we all need to
come to God and repent and be Saved before we can ever get to heaven
and again Ralph is my child and i Know he is not what he ought to be but
has Strayed a way and went against my will but we are praying that Some
day he will come back and give his heart to God So may the Lord help you
to See and to Think as This was your child Sincerely your friend Ga Cave[1]
PS please let me hear from you

1. See also the letters of March 26, June 5 and 14, and December 1, 1937, and February 5 and 10 and November 3, 1938.

[received Apr 2 1938]   Mr Lacy Taylor   Fletcher, Va

Dear Sir.

I was given permission to occupy the Pleasant Snow Place an I havent
farm any land only that had Ben cultivated an I have only one corn an any
fence is in Bad condition around my corn field an other little garden spots
an some people out of the Park want to turn their cattle an horses in an
they will get in my crops an destroy it an if you Please rite and let me

know if I can keep them out ar not you rite an let me know at once. Yours Very Truely

Lacy Taylor

~~~

April 4.19.38.   Nethers. Va.

dear mr Lassiter i am ritting to You to see if You Will give me a per mit to stay Here till fall as it is getting verry late and i dont now if they Have got me a Home yet or not and if they get the wone that they Have picked out they will Have to Build me a House and that will make it a Bout the first of May Before i can move and you now that it will Be to late to make any thing then i dont see where it will make the matter any worse to let me stay and farm some gardens as i now i never Has give you all any trouble so please let me Hear from you at Wonce

Yours truley
EB. Nicholson[1]
Nethers. Va

1. Ephraim B. Nicholson. See also the letters of March 13, 1936, and April 18 and May 1, 1938.

~~~

Leon, Va.   4/13/1938

Mr. Pop Foster,
Dear Sir:

the lady who works under the directions of mrs. Humrickhouse was here monday and she said I had a perfect right to that lumber which Mr. Lassiter gave me at the school house, and she said that she meant to furnish new lumber to repair what the old lumber lacked, or in other words to furnish new, if the old were not enough to do all of the repair work here. If it has not been hauled away yet, Please bring it on down here at once. We need it very bad. I am sorry that there seemed to be a misunderstanding with Mr. Hoskins about this. I hope you will see to this matter at once. Richard worked hard getting that pile of lumber out and yet may not get the benifit of it. Please bring me at once at least one truck load of

the best of that pile also about 25 of those 2 by 4 in that pile which lies by
the pile of lumber. We need it to build a little house over the Spring to
keep the milk and butter in. Please do your best to get this for me.

   Mr. Hoskins also said he would have me 2 loads of wood hauled. I have
had one load so far. Mr. Foster, Please get after him about this, and especially the lumber. Will appreciate it very much in deed.

Yours

Mrs. Teeny Florence Nicholson,[1]

Leon, Va.

   1. By this time, Nicholson had moved from her mountain home to Leon in
Madison County. See also the letters of December 29, 1934, and March 8 and 26 and
August 7, 1938.

April.18.19.38   Nethers Va

Well Mr Lassiter Just a line to see what is the reason you did not ans the
letter i rote you some time a go asking you a Bout farming my gardens
Her so it is time to make gardin and if i dont Hear something Buy the 21
of this month i am going to make garden Here Just as always so i want to
Hear from you not later than the 21 as i cant Be starved to dith Yours
truly

E.B. Nicholson[1]

   1. Ephraim B. Nicholson. See also the letters of March 13, 1936, and April 4 and
May 1, 1938.

May 1.1938   Nethers Va

dear mr Lassiter i will rite you a gain to see What is the reason you do not
ans none of my letters as this is 3 times i Have rote you a Bout getting
Word to farm my gardens and cant Hear nothing so you now that it is
time long a go to of Ben made garden as i Have Had my son to Break up
my garden and i am ritting to you you can let me now to tell you if you
dont let me now on or Before Wednesday may the 4 iam going to plant
some garden as i do not want any trouble a Bout this mater and it will

soon Be to late to plant any thing and then What do you think i will do as if i dont raise a little something i Will Be Bound to starve to dith on what little iam getting so i now you can let me now Buy Wednesday May the 4 you can let me now Buy wone of the Raingers

Yours truley

EB. Nicholson[1]

Nethers. Va.

1. See also the letters of March 13, 1936, and April 4 and 18, 1938.

～～～

Kimball Va   June. 9 1938

Mr Lastor the park rangers was here yestrday and said I had to have them cattle out in 6 days. I cant get them out in 6 days But you give me 30 days I will have them all out. one will come and tell me one thing a nother will come and tell me a nother thing so I dont know what to do. so I want some information from you I have a Big Family and a poor Man. no way to make a Living

   I did not see him my self

Henry Jewell

Kimball Va.

～～～

Leon. Va.   Aug 7, 1938

Mr. J.R. Lassiter

Luray Va.

My Dear Mr. Lassiter,

I am writing you for a permit for my apples at the old mountain house. I understand the home Steads at Wolf Town is geting apples from the park and is selling them so I will be very thankfull if you can let me have them Thanking you for your kindness in the past. I am

Respt

Mrs Teeny F. Nicholson[1]

1. See also the letters of December 29, 1934; March 13, 1937; and March 8 and 26 and April 13, 1938.

aug 12 1938   Skyland Va

dear mr lassier ie [I] wanted to see if you wood give me apermit for apart
of those apples where i live at ada dodson people seams to think that we
dont have iny rite to them when wavley T dyer[1] lived here hea got fruit
of the place Just as Same as his father got we lived on the same place that
ada lives an and dont you think that we have just as much right to a of the
aples as the do an mr lassier i wanted to ast you about apermit an John
dyers place the wavley dyer place is gat apermit for last winter, att [that]
familys is destraid [destroyed] about all of the fruit there and ada
dads / wife sed we can not get iny apples where i do live so John dyers
place is wright at us so please send me apemit for the apples at Johns place
    ie have got nine little children to take cear of and Mr lassier ie wanted
to explan afew more things to you when we left our old home place last
winter to come to the wavleys T dyers place that we got apermit for we
had some peach trees at our home place my husmand Baught the trees at
tended to them and never has Been iny peaches on them tell this year and
my humand tale ada dad and willie dad and Eranest dad not to Bother
them tell the got ripe he wood give them apart of thim and the went in
afew days after that and gat all af the peaches and wood iet Bee ok ief iera
Brown wood look after the ather apples an wavley dyers other place that
we gat apermit for he livs near to them than we do ather peaple ies de-
straning [destroying] all of the green friut iera Brown sed he wood try
and look after the place for us ief iet wood Bee all right with you and now
have do you think had the most wright to them us or them we had all of
the trouble with the peachs trees and all so the Broke down the green
trees so you send me arite for afew of the apples where we ar living at no
and John dyers place ie Just want afew for family use mr lassier willie dad
has aachet [orchard] an his place and all so he sed that he had a permit
for tiney place and all so the get apples af in John dyer place and we have
no apples far family youse [use] and ada dads wife sed we Should not get
iny of the place where we live so you please give me apermit for Johns apples and all so for herburt dyers aples[2]

1. Waverly T. Dyer.
2. This letter is not signed, but it is located in the Charley Dyer folder and the

handwriting is similar to other letters signed by Mrs. Charley Dyer, that is, Lizzie Nicholson Dyer. See also the letters of April 10 and May 8, 1936, and the letters signed "Charley Dyer" or "Charles E. Dyer" dated April 8, 1936; November 5, 1937; and March 14, 1938.

~~~

Stanley, Va   November 3

dear Mr Haskins
as you Said you was going to have that Doctor bill Setteled but i have a nother bill from Dr Ross that it has never been Setteled So i would love for you to See to it iff you possibly Can as i have had no work for a long time and the boy is not in any Camp now So please do what you Can

Sincrely G a Cave[1]

1. See also the letters of March 26, June 5 and 14, and December 1, 1937, and February 5 and 10 and April 1, 1938.

~~~

Stanley Va   Nov 19 1938

Dear sir Mr Lassiter
I am writting you about my pattoes which I planted at my old home place and had arders do so By Mr Hirrman Ranger and also Mr Hoskin and Mr Hirman was to See me about them and he Said he would fix it with me about them Camp no 3 destroyed them I planted 2 dollars worth Seed and they was very good Ef you want to you can Send Some Body to Eastamate about what it would Been worth I am a widdow and worked hard for them I feel like you or willing to get me Somphing for them

yours Truly
Lilla Meadows[1]
Tanners Ridge
Stanley Va

1. Lilla Meadows, who was married to Robert Eldon Meadows, owned twenty-one acres on tract 424 in Page County, land that was surveyed but not purchased for the park.

Matilda Breeden, a
Greene County
resident given life
tenure in Shenandoah
National Park, on her
front porch writing in
1946. (Courtesy of
Shenandoah National
Park Archives; used
by permission of
Breeden's family)

[no date, stamped "1938" by SNP]

DEAR SIR i AM ASKiNG A FAVOR OF YOU iHAV A HOG TO KILL
AND HAV NO PLAC TO SALT MY MEAT i WOULD BE AFUL
GLAD iF YOU WOULD PUT ME UP JUST A SMALL BiLDEN TO
PUT MY MEAT IN. MY HOUSE iS SO SMALL iHAV NO ROOM
iHAV NO UP STAiRS TO PUT ANY THiNG JUST THREE ROOMS
AND HAV THEM FULL THEiR ARE ALMOST LUMBER ENOUGH
HEAR TO PUT UP A SMALL BiLDEN YOURS VERY TRULY
FROM MATiLDA BREEDEN[1] ONE YOU CALL CASE i AM ALSO
OUT OF WOOD AND NO WHER TO GET ANY

1. Matilda Breeden, together with George and Ellen Hurt and John R. and Elizabeth Nicholson, was granted life tenure and remained in the park until 1946, when
she moved elsewhere.

Remaining Concerns and Revising Eminent Domain Laws

After the last of the families, except for those few granted life tenure, were moved from the park, several letters trickled into the park's headquarters in Luray over the years. Some of these letters were written by descendants of former residents of the park, requesting information about their families and photographs. Some descendants provided photographs and family information to be included in the park's archives. Still other letters were written by nearby residents requesting to pick blueberries or to remove dead wood, practices that the park now consistently restricts.

The following five examples highlight several residents' attempts to continue to live in the park or to understand park policy regarding their previous homes. These letters reflect the ways that the park had and continues to have an enormous impact on the families and communities that were displaced. In one letter, Richard Nicholson asked Senator Byrd for help in petitioning for families to be able to return to their homes. Nicholson's plea, which came nearly ten years after his family's relocation, illustrates the last glimmer of hope that residents held that their situations could be remedied. Nicholson's letter was politely answered, but of course no one was allowed back in the park. The letters written by Barbara Nicholson and Buck Dodson are similar to Matilda Breeden's in 1938. As a life-tenure resident, Barbara Nicholson relied on the park's rangers for assistance. Similarly, Dodson asked for assistance from the park since his windows were originally obtained from his home in the park. Helen Jeffries, a local attorney, wrote in advocacy for Tenie Atkins, an appeal that prompted the Park Service to grant Atkins life tenure. Atkins later wrote to Superintendent Granville Liles informing him of her intention to leave the park. This letter, written in 1950, illustrates the way that the park continued to affect residents' lives and shows that a formal letter was necessary to end her living arrangements.

~~~

Helen M. Jeffries   Attorney at Law   Culpeper, VA.

November 28th, 1939,
Shenandoah National Park Service
Luray, Virginia.
Dear Sir:

About a month ago I was in your office and asked about the proper party to see about the moving of Miss Teeny Adkins from the Park Area near Sperryville. I was advised to see the Chief Ranger who had an office at Elkton. Due to the snow that day I did not go but after returning to Culpeper to put a long distance call in to Elkton and I was advised that no office was at Elkton.

I am going to state the case and you in turn can turn this letter over to the proper party. Miss Teeny Adkins has a piece of property just within the Park Area near Sperryville, Virginia. She tells me that she is supposed to move but that she has no place to move to. She has been to see me about a place I own near Amissville, Virginia and she tells me that the Government has been buying places and moving people to them. I do not know anything about it and she asked me to get in touch with a Mr. Fox and he would tell me about it.

Miss Teeny Adkins was not the sole owner of the place she now lives on and the proceeds of the money received from her place will not buy her another home. She lives with her brother and she wants to move as soon as a place can be provided. I do not know her very well and it has just been since she looked at my place that she has asked me to find out what the Government is going to do about moving her.

I will appreciate some information from you relative to this matter. I did not know the government was buying property for the epople who were moving off but Miss Adkins insists she is not going to move until a place is provided for her.

Very truly yours,
Helen M. Jeffries[1]

1. Jeffries's letter, like those of Wiley R. Mason (November 19, 1934, and March 19 and December 5, 1935) and Janet Walton (June 8 and December 4, 1935), is an example of the kind of advocacy that occurred as community members sought to help park residents. By seeking the support of the attorneys, residents such as Atkins positioned themselves as having worthy cases to be heard by the community and the government. Jeffries's letter prompted a series of subsequent letters among park officials, the Department of Public Welfare, and the Department of the Interior, discussing Atkins's case for life-tenure residency. The director of the National Park Service, Arno Cammerer, said in his letter of February 23, 1940, "The Acting Superintendent [Lassiter] advises that miss Atkins has never given any trouble to the park. . . . It is recommended that the present list of aged persons permitted to remain in Shenandoah National Park for the rest of their lives be revised as suggested by the Acting Superintendent, by adding the name of Miss Teeny Atkins." Atkins was granted life tenure on the basis of the initial advocacy of Helen Jeffries. See Atkins's letter of October 26, 1950 (on p. 160).

<center>~~~~~</center>

August 7, 1945.   Leon, Va.

Mr. Harry F. Byrd,
Winchester, Va.
My dear Mr. Byrd:

   I received your letter of July 31st and was glad to note that you will make full inquiry into the matter concerning the Government letting the people go back to their homes in the mountains. Mr. Byrd, a number of mountain people have asked me to write and ask you if it would do any good or be a chance whatever of the people getting their homes back to have petitions wrote out and lay these petitions before Congress on the grounds that the mountain people was badly misled when they sold their land for a park believing that they could stay there and not be forced to move. Almost every man or woman who moved from the park would sign such a petition. There is those who live in different homestead locations and 9 out of 10 would much rather go back to their old home in the mountains. Because they were born and reared in the mountains and they will never be satisfied otherwise. I will be very glad if you will give me this information. Also if the move mentioned above would do any good send me a sample as to how such petitions should be wrote or fixed up. The mountain people and myself will be awfully thankful for anything you can do or suggest in this matter. Hoping to hear from you soon,

Respectfully yours,
Richard Nicholson[1]

1. See also the letters of November 11, 1935, and August 10, 1936, and the letters written by Richard's mother, Teeny Florence Corbin Nicholson, dated December 29, 1934, and March 8 and 26, April 13, and August 7, 1938.

<center>~~~~~</center>

Syria Va.   Jan. 3, 1946

Ranger Weelden

Dear Sir

I am writing you to say, I am all most out of wood wish you would send me a load at once, thanking you,

Barbara Nicholson[1]
Syria, Va.

1. Mrs. William Aldridge Nicholson. See also her letters of 1935 (no date; end of the year) and February 5, 1937.

<center>~~~~~</center>

Amissville, Virginia   October 26, 1950

Superintendent[1]

Shenandoah National Park

Luray, Virginia

Dear Sir:

I do not intend to return to the old Jonos Atkins place where Frank (Dido) Atkins now dwells and wish that you would move him out, to live with Lee Atkins.

Please do what you can to have Welfare Department of Rappahonnock County arrange for him to live with Lee Atkins satisfactorily.

I left the old home in April 1941 and will never return so wish you to tear down the place so that there will be no more trouble there.

Very truly yours,
Tenie Atkins Darnell[2]

1. Atkins's letter does not specify the superintendent's name. Granville Liles was acting superintendent from October 15, 1950, to January 6, 1951. Edward D. Freeland was superintendent (after Lassiter) from January 1, 1942, to October 14, 1950.

2. The "Jonos Atkins place" to which Tenie refers was the forty-one acres on tract 175 in Rappahannock County that he owned and for which he was paid $1,592 by the state.

November, 8. 1951   Winston, Virginia

Dear Mr. E. R. McKesson.
Dear Sir:

I am writing to see if you could help me with my window sashes they are not any good the bad weather has done runt them, I would like for them to be fixed before cold weather, so my fruit wont freeze. Also I would like to have the house painted it needs painting bad, It would help to save it also.

We dont have any deed to the house it belong to the govenment but we would like for you to have it fixed. Write back at once and let me no if you will fix the windows.

Yours Truley
Buck Dodson.[1]
Winston, Virginia
R.FD. #.1 Bx 69

1. James Walker "Buck" Dodson. See also the letters of March 24 and September 8, 1936.

Many families who left the park found their own alternative housing. Some moved into one of the seven resettlement communities that were part of the Shenandoah Homesteads Project operated by the Resettlement Administration (and later by the Farm Security Administration). The seven communities included Elkton in Rockingham County, Flint Hill and Washington in Rappahannock County, Geer in Greene County, Ida Valley in Page County, and Madison and Wolftown in Madison County. For some residents, a sense of community was maintained in these communities, but their livelihoods were mostly drastically changed, as their small farm subsistence living shifted to small tract houses in close proximity to neighbors.

Among the people who live in close proximity to the park and who are descendants of the displaced residents, there remain mixed feelings about SNP. There is a sense of pride about the beauty of the park and about their families' legacies in its history, yet there are also remnants of bitterness. Their families were forced to move, their land condemned for the so-called broader public good, and their lives were changed forever unwillingly.

The story of displacement from SNP resonates today, as U.S. citizens' homes continue to be condemned for public use, for such uses as road expansion and building and public utilities. The Fifth Amendment of the U.S. Constitution states, "nor shall private property be taken for public use without just compensation." With the Public Park Condemnation Act of 1928, the Commonwealth of Virginia determined that taking private citizens' lands for a park constituted public use and that it could therefore legally force landowners to sell for the just compensation of a "fair market price." What constitutes "public use" has long been contested in the United States, and on June 23, 2005, the U.S. Supreme Court made a landmark eminent domain decision that sent states scrambling to reexamine their condemnation laws. Based on the case of *Kelo v. New London, Connecticut,* private developers can now argue for their economic development projects as "public purpose," essentially making all "takings" by states justifiable— even if those takings benefit private citizens or companies. That case has caused many states to take great pause as they consider whether their own condemnation laws adequately protect landowners from takings by other private parties.

The stories collected here, as told in the words of the displaced people themselves, might serve as cautionary tales about the enormous psychological, economic, political, and social impacts of displacing families. Although widening roads and obtaining land for other public-use projects may arguably count as being for the public good, *how* those lands are obtained and *how* the displaced people are compensated and treated during that displacement matters.

Bibliography

Anglin, Mary K. *Women, Power, and Dissent in the Hills of Carolina*. Urbana: University of Illinois Press, 2002.

Appalachian Land Ownership Task Force. *Who Owns Appalachia? Landownership and Its Impact*. Lexington: University Press of Kentucky, 1983.

Aron, Cindy S. *Working at Play: A History of Vacations in the United States*. Oxford: Oxford University Press, 1999.

Baghban, Marcia. "The Application of Culturally Relevant Factors to Literacy Programs in Appalachia." *Reading-Horizons* 24.2 (Winter 1984): 75–82.

Barber, Alicia. "Local Places, National Spaces: Public Memory, Community Identity, and Landscape at Scotts Bluff National Monument." *American Studies* 45.2 (Summer 2004): 35–64.

Beaver, Patricia Duane. *Rural Community in the Appalachian South*. Lexington: University Press of Kentucky, 1986.

Becker, Jane S. *Selling Tradition: Appalachia and the Construction of an American Folk, 1930–1940*. Chapel Hill: University of North Carolina Press, 1998.

Bender, Margaret, ed. *Linguistic Diversity in the South: Changing Codes, Practices, and Ideology*. Athens: University of Georgia Press, 2004.

———. *Signs of Cherokee Culture: Sequoyah's Syllabary in Eastern Cherokee Life*. Chapel Hill: University of North Carolina Press, 2006.

Billings, Dwight B. Introduction to *Confronting Appalachian Stereotypes: Back Talk from an American Region*. Edited by Dwight B. Billings, Gurney Norman, and Katherine Ledford. Lexington: University Press of Kentucky, 1999. 3–20.

Billings, Dwight B., and Kathleen Blee. *The Road to Poverty: The Making of Wealth and Hardship in Appalachia*. Cambridge: Cambridge University Press, 2000.

Billings, Dwight B., Gurney Norman, and Katherine Ledford, eds. *Confronting Appalachian Stereotypes: Back Talk from an American Region*. Lexington: University Press of Kentucky, 1999.

Bradshaw, Michael. *The Appalachian Regional Commission: Twenty-Five Years of Government Policy*. Lexington: University Press of Kentucky, 1992.

Brooke, Robert, ed. *Rural Voices: Place-Conscious Education and the Teaching of Writing*. New York: Teachers College Press, 2003.

Campbell, John C. *The Southern Highlander and His Homeland*. New York: Russell Sage Foundation, 1921.

Carr, Ethan. *Wilderness by Design*. Lincoln: University of Nebraska Press, 1998.

Chandler, William U. *The Myth of TVA: Conservation and Development in the Tennessee Valley, 1933–1983.* Cambridge, MA: Ballinger, 1984.

Cohen, Robert, ed. *Dear Mrs. Roosevelt: Letters from Children of the Great Depression.* Chapel Hill: University of North Carolina Press, 2002.

Crane, Suzanne. "Teaching Advanced Research Techniques to Community College Students: Examining the Eviction of Mountain Residents from the Shenandoah National Park." *Inquiry* 1.2 (Fall 1997): 40–43.

Dabney, Virginius. *Virginia: The New Dominion: A History from 1607 to the Present.* Charlottesville: University Press of Virginia, 1971.

Dannenberg, Clare, and Walt Wolfram. "Ethnic Identity and Grammatical Restructuring: Be(s)in Lumbee English." *American Speech* 73 (February 1999): 139–59.

Decker, William Merrill. *Epistolary Practices: Letter Writing in America before Telecommunications.* Chapel Hill: University of North Carolina Press, 1998.

Donehower, Kim. "Rhetorics and Realities: The History and Effects of Stereotypes about Rural Literacies." In *Rural Literacies.* Carbondale: Southern Illinois University Press, 2007. 37–76.

Drake, Richard B. *A History of Appalachia.* Lexington: University Press of Kentucky, 2001.

———. "Slavery and Antislavery in Appalachia." In *Appalachians and Race: The Mountain South from Slavery to Segregation.* Edited by John C. Inscoe. Lexington: University Press of Kentucky, 2001. 16–26.

Dunn, Durwood. *Cades Cove: The Life and Death of a Southern Appalachian Community, 1918–1937.* Knoxville: University of Tennessee Press, 1988.

Dyer, Joyce. ed. *Bloodroot: Reflections on Place by Appalachian Women Writers.* Lexington: University Press of Kentucky, 2000.

Eller, Ronald D. *Miners, Millhands, and Mountaineers: Industrialization of the Appalachian South, 1880–1930.* Knoxville: University of Tennessee Press, 1982.

Engle, Reed. *Everything Was Wonderful: A Pictorial History of the Civilian Conservation Corps in Shenandoah National Park.* Luray, VA: Shenandoah Natural History Association, 1999.

———. *The Greatest Single . . . A Sky-Line Drive.* Luray, VA: Shenandoah National Park Association Press, 2006.

———. "Segregation/Desegration: Laboratory for Change." Shenandoah National Park website. January 1996. www.nps.gov/shen/historyculture/segregation.htm (accessed February 4, 2009).

———. "Shenandoah National Park: A Historical Overview." *Cultural Resource Management* 21.1 (1998): 9.

———. "

Skyline Drive: A Road to Nowhere?" Shenandoah National Park website. October 6, 2004. www.nps.gov/shen/3b2a2.htm (accessed July 7, 2005).

Engle, Reed L., and Caroline Janney. *A Database of Shenandoah National Park Land Records.* Luray, VA: Shenandoah National Park, 1997.

Ewald, Wendy. *Portraits and Dreams and Appalachia: A Self-Portrait.* Frankfort, KY: Gnomon, 1979.

Findley, Warren. "Musicians and Mountaineers: The Resettlement Administration in Appalachia." *Appalachian Journal*, 1979, 105–23.

Fisher, Stephen L., ed. *Fighting Back in Appalachia: Traditions of Resistance and Change*. Philadelphia: Temple University Press, 1993.

Fordney, Chris. "Boundary Wars." *National Parks* 70.1–2 (January 1996): 24–34.

Foster, Stephen. *The Past Is Another Country: Representation, Historical Consciousness, and Resistance in the Blue Ridge*. Berkeley: University of California Press, 1988.

Gaventa, John. "The Political Economy of Land Tenure: Appalachia and the Southeast." In *Who Owns America? Social Conflict over Property Rights*. Edited by Harvey M. Jacobs. Madison: University of Wisconsin Press, 1998. 227–44.

———. *Power and Powerlessness: Quiescence and Rebellion in an Appalachian Valley*. Oxford, UK: Clarendon, 1980.

Gaventa, John, Barbara Ellen Smith, and Alex Willingham, eds. *Communities in Economic Crisis: Appalachia and the South*. Philadelphia: Temple University Press, 1990.

Green, Elna C. *This Business of Relief: Confronting Poverty in a Southern City, 1740–1940*. Athens: University of Georgia Press, 2003.

———. Introduction to *The New Deal and Beyond: Social Welfare in the South since 1930*. Edited by Elna C. Green. Athens: University of Georgia Press, 2003. vii–xix.

The Ground Beneath Our Feet. Companion Web site for documentary series. www.vahistory.org. Designed by William G. Thomas III.

Hazen, Kirk, and Ellen Fluharty. "Defining Appalachian English." In *Linguistic Diversity in the South: Changing Codes, Practices, and Ideology*. Edited by Margaret Bender. Athens: University of Georgia Press, 2004. 50–65.

Heinemann, Ronald L. *Depression and New Deal in Virginia: The Enduring Dominion*. Charlottesville: University Press of Virginia, 1983.

———. *Harry Byrd of Virginia*. Charlottesville: University Press of Virginia, 1996.

Henderson, Henry L., and David B. Woolner, eds. *FDR and the Environment*. New York: Palgrave Macmillan, 2005.

Horning, Audrey. "Archeological Considerations of 'Appalachian' Identity." In *The Archeology of Communities: A New World Perspective*. Edited by Marcello A. Canuto and Jason Yaeger. London: Routledge, 2000. 210–30.

———. "Beyond the Shenandoah Valley: Interaction, Image, and Identity in the Blue Ridge." In *After the Backcountry: Rural Life in the Great Valley of Virginia 1800–1900*. Edited by Kenneth E. Koons and Warren R. Hofstra. Knoxville: University of Tennessee Press, 2000. 145–66.

———. *In the Shadow of Ragged Mountain: Historical Archaeology of Nicholson, Corbin, and Weakley Hollows*. Luray, VA: Shenandoah National Park Association, 2004.

Inscoe, John, ed. *Appalachians and Race: The Mountain South from Slavery to Segregation*. Lexington: University Press of Kentucky, 2001.

———. "Race and Racism in Nineteenth-Century Southern Appalachia: Myths, Realities, and Ambiguities." In *Appalachia in the Making: The Mountain South in the Nineteenth Century*. Edited by Mary Beth Pudup, Dwight Billings, and Altina Waller. Chapel Hill: University of North Carolina Press, 1995. 103–31.

Janney-Lucas, Carrie. "Why Not Panorama?" Shenandoah National Park website. July 2, 2004. www.nps.gov/shen/whynotpanorma.htm (accessed July 7, 2005).

Jolley, Harley E. *The Blue Ridge Parkway.* Knoxville: University of Tennessee Press, 1969.

Kahn, Kathy. *Hillbilly Women.* Garden City, NY: Doubleday, 1972.

Kephart, Horace. *Our Southern Highlanders.* New York: Outing, 1913.

Knepper, Cathy D. *Dear Mrs. Roosevelt: Letters to Eleanor Roosevelt through Depression and War.* New York: Carroll and Graf, 2004.

Krutko, Erin. "Lewis Mountain: Signs of Segregation in Shenandoah National Park." Paper presented at the Designing the National Parks Conference, University of Virginia, Charlottesville, May 2008.

Lambert, Darwin. *The Undying Past of Shenandoah National Park.* Boulder, CO: Roberts Rienhart, 1989.

Lassiter, James R. *Shenandoah National Park.* Richmond, VA: Commonwealth, 1936.

Lewis, Ronald L. *Transforming the Appalachian Countryside: Railroads, Deforestation, and Social Change in West Virginia, 1880–1920.* Chapel Hill: University of North Carolina Press, 1998.

Link, William A. *A Hard Country and a Lonely Place: Schooling, Society, and Reform in Rural Virginia, 1870–1920.* Chapel Hill: University of North Carolina Press, 1986.

Mackintosh, Barry. "The National Park Service: A Brief History." National Park Service website. www.cr.nps.gov/history/hisnps/NPSHistory/npshisto.htm (accessed August 20, 2004).

Maggard, Sally Ward. "Coalfield Women Making History." In *Confronting Stereotypes in Appalachia: Backtalk from an American Region.* Edited by Dwight Billings, Gurney Norman, and Katherine Ledford. Lexington: University Press of Kentucky, 1999. 228–50.

———. "Gender, Race, Place: Confounding Labor Activism in Central Appalachia." In *Neither Separate nor Equal: Women, Race, and Class in the South.* Edited by Barbara Ellen Smith. Philadelphia: Temple University Press, 1999. 185–206.

Maher, Neil M. "'A Conflux of Desire and Need': Trees, Boy Scouts, and the Roots of Franklin Roosevelt's Civilian Conservation Corps." In *FDR and the Environment.* Edited by Henderson, Henry L. and David B. Woolner. New York: Palgrave Macmillan, 2005. 49–84.

———. *Nature's New Deal: The Civilian Conservation Corps and the Roots of the American Environmental Movement.* Oxford: Oxford University Press, 2007.

Martin-Perdue, Nancy J., and Charles L. Perdue Jr., eds. *Talk about Trouble: A New Deal Portrait of Virginians in the Great Depression.* Chapel Hill: University of North Carolina Press, 1996.

McDonald, Michael J., and John Muldowney. *TVA and the Dispossessed.* Knoxville: University of Tennessee Press, 1982.

McElvaine, Robert. *Down and Out in the Great Depression: Letters from the Forgotten Man.* Chapel Hill: University of North Carolina Press, 1983.

McGuffey, William H. *The McGuffey Reader: McGuffey's Rhetorical Guide; Fifth Reader; The Eclectic Series containing elegant extracts in prose and poetry with copious rules and rhetorical exercises.* New York: Clark, Austin, and Smith, 1844.

McNeil, W. K., ed. *Appalachian Images in Folk and Popular Culture.* Knoxville: University of Tennessee Press, 1995.

Meltz, Robert. *When the United States Takes Property: Legal Principles.* Washington, DC: Congressional Research Service Report, 1991.

Merrifield, Juliet, Mary Beth Bingman, David Hemphill, and Kathleen Bennett deMarrais. *Life at the Margins: Literacy, Language, and Technology in Everyday Life.* New York: Teachers College Press, 1997.

Mills, Henry E. *A Treatise upon the Law of Eminent Domain.* St. Louis: F. H. Thomas and Company, 1879.

Montell, William Lynwood. *The Saga of Coe Ridge: A Study in Oral History.* Knoxville: University of Tennessee Press, 1970.

Montgomery, Michael. "In the Appalachians They Speak Like Shakespeare." In *Language Myths.* Edited by Laurie Bauer and Peter Trudgill. New York: Penguin, 1998. 66–76.

——. "The Scotch-Irish Element in Appalachian English: How Broad? How Deep?" In *Ulster and North America: Transatlantic Perspectives on the Scotch-Irish.* Edited by H. Blethen and C. Wood. Tuscaloosa: University of Alabama Press, 1997. 189–212.

Mortensen, Peter. "Representations of Literacy and Region: Narrating 'Another America.'" In *Pedagogy in the Age of Politics: Writing and Reading (in) the Academy.* Edited by Patricia A. Sullivan and Donna J. Qualley. Urbana, IL: National Council of Teachers of English, 1994. 100–120.

Nicholson, John T. "The Old Mountain Home. *Madison County Eagle.* June 1, 1934.

Northern Virginia Park Association. "A National Park Near the Nation's Capital: Information Bulletin." Page, VA: Northern Virginia Park Association, 1924. In Resource Management Records, Ferdenand Zerkel Papers, box 2, folder 10, Shenandoah National Park Archives, Luray, Virginia.

Nowak, Liesel. "Exhibit Explores Displaced Lives." *Daily Progress* (Charlottesville, VA). August 2, 2004.

O'Connor, Justice Sandra Day. "Dissenting Opinion of the Court." *Susette Kelo, et al., Petitioners v. City of New London, Connecticut.* 545 U.S., No. 04–108. June 23, 2005.

Olson, Ted. *Blue Ridge Folklife.* Jackson: University Press of Mississippi, 1998.

——. "In the Public Interest? The Social and Cultural Impact of the Blue Ridge Parkway, a Depression-Era Appalachian 'Public Works' Project." In *The New Deal and Beyond: Social Welfare in the South since 1930.* Edited by Elna C. Green. Athens: University of Georgia Press, 2003. 100–115.

Pasternak, Donna L. "Learning Tolerant Practice in Appalachia." *Profession* (Modern Language Association), 2003, 94–104.

Perdue, Charles, and Nancy Perdue. "Appalachian Fables and Facts." *Appalachian Journal,* Autumn/Winter 1979–80, 84–104.

——. "'To Build a Wall around These Mountains': The Displaced People of Shenandoah." *Magazine of Albemarle County History* 49 (1991): 48–71.

Pluckett, John. *Foxfire Reconsidered: A Twenty-Year Experiment in Progressive Education.* Urbana: University of Illinois Press, 1989.

Pollock, George Freeman. "Answer to Government Questionnaire Concerning Proposed Southern Appalachian National Park." Ferdenand Zerkel Papers, box 6, folder 1, Shenandoah National Park Archives, Luray, Virginia.

——. *Skyland: The Heart of the Shenandoah National Park.* Edited by Stuart E. Brown, Jr. Berryville, VA: Chesapeake Book Company, 1960.

Powell, Katrina M. *The Anguish of Displacement: The Politics of Literacy in the Letters of Mountain Families in Shenandoah National Park.* Charlottesville: University of Virginia Press, 2007.

——. "Virginia Women Writing to Government Officials: Letters of Request as Social Participation." In *Women and Literacy: Local and Global Inquiries for a New Century.* Edited by Beth Daniell and Peter Mortensen. NCTE-LEA Research Series in Literacy and Composition. New York: Lawrence Erlbaum Associates, 2007. 71–90.

——. "Writing the Geography of the Blue Ridge Mountains: How Displacement Recorded the Land." *Biography: An Interdisciplinary Journal* 25.1 (Winter 2002): 73–94.

Public Park Condemnation Act of the General Assembly of Virginia. March 22, 1928.

Puckett, Anita. "Identity, Hybridity, and Linguistic Ideologies of Racial Language in the Upper South." In *Linguistic Diversity in the South: Changing Codes, Practices, and Ideology.* Edited by Margaret Bender. Athens: University of Georgia Press, 2004. 120–37.

——. "'Let the Girls Do the Spelling and Dan Will Do the Shooting': Literacy, the Division of Labor, and Identity in a Rural Appalachian Community." *Anthropological Quarterly* 65.3 (July 1992): 137–47.

——. "The Melungeon Identity Movement and the Construction of Appalachian Whiteness." *Journal of Linguistic Anthropology* 11.1 (2001): 131–46.

Pudup, Mary Beth, Dwight B. Billings, and Altina L. Waller, eds. *Appalachia in the Making: The Mountain South in the Nineteenth Century.* Chapel Hill: University of North Carolina Press, 1995.

Reeder, Carolyn, and Jack Reeder. *Shenandoah Heritage: The Story of the People before the Park.* Washington, DC: Potomac Appalachian Trail Club, 1978.

——. *Shenandoah Secrets: The Story of the Park's Hidden Past.* Washington, DC: Potomac Appalachian Trail Club, 1991.

——. *Shenandoah Vestiges: What the Mountain People Left Behind.* Washington, DC: Potomac Appalachian Trail Club, 1980.

Reynolds, George P. "The CCC: The Road to Recovery." In *Foxfire 10.* New York: Anchor Books, 1993. 240–302.

Roe, Charles E. "Use of Conservation Easements to Protect the Scenic and Natural Character of the Blue Ridge Parkway: A Case Study." In *Protecting the Land: Con-*

servation Easements Past, Present, and Future. Edited by Julie Ann Gustanski and Roderick H. Squires. Washington, DC: Island, 2000. 221–29.

Salstrom, Paul. *Appalachia's Path to Dependency: Rethinking a Region's Economic History, 1730–1940.* Lexington: University Press of Kentucky, 1994.

Schultz, Lucille M. "Letter-Writing Instruction in 19th Century Schools in the United States." In *Letter Writing as Social Practice.* Edited by David Barton and Nigel Hall. Amsterdam: John Benjamins, 1999. 109–30.

Sexton, Roy. "The Forgotten People of the Shenandoah." *America Civic Annual* 2 (1930): 19–22.

Shands, William E. *The Subdivision of Virginia's Mountains: The Environmental Impact of Recreation Subdivision in the Massanutten Mountain—Blue Ridge Area, Virginia: A Survey and Report.* Washington, DC: Central Atlantic Environment Center, 1974.

Shapiro, Henry D. *Appalachia on Our Minds: The Southern Mountains and Mountaineer in the American Consciousness, 1870–1920.* Chapel Hill: University of North Carolina Press, 1978.

Shenandoah, The Gift. Film produced by Harpers Ferry Center, NPS, U.S. Department of Interior. Directed by Shawn Freude. Executive producer and narrator George H. Gilliam.

Sherman, Mandel, and Thomas Henry. *Hollow Folk.* New York: Thomas Crowell and Company, 1933.

Simmons, Dennis Elwood. "Conservation, Cooperation, and Controversy: The Establishment of Shenandoah National Park, 1924–1936." *Virginia Magazine of History and Biography* 89.4 (October 1981): 115–35.

———. "The Creation of the Shenandoah National Park and the Skyline Drive." Ph.D. diss., University of Virginia, 1978.

Sizer, Miriam. "Suggestions Concerning Some Types of Mountain People in the Proposed Shenandoah National Park." Shenandoah National Park Papers, National Archives Satellite, College Park, Maryland, n.d.

———. "Tabulations." Shenandoah National Park Papers, National Archives Satelitte, College Park, Maryland, 1932.

Skocpol, Theda. *Protecting Soldiers and Mothers: The Political Origins of Social Policy in the United States.* Cambridge, MA: Belknap Press of Harvard University Press, 1992.

Smith, Barbara Ellen. " 'Beyond the Mountains': The Paradox of Women's Place in Appalachian History." *National Women's Studies Association Journal* 11.3 (1999): 1–17.

———. "De-gradations of Whiteness: Appalachia and the Complexities of Race." *Journal of Appalachian Studies* 10.1–2 (2004): 38–57.

Smith, Dorothy Noble. *Recollections: The People of the Blue Ridge Remember.* Verona, VA: McClure, 1983.

Smith, Leef. "Anger in Appalachia: Researchers Fighting to Open Records on 1930s Shenandoah Park Settlement." *Washington Post.* March 6, 2000.

Sohn, Katherine Kelleher. "Whistlin' and Crowin' Women of Appalachia: Literacy Practices since College." *College Composition and Communication* 54 (2003): 423–52.

Stevens, John Paul. "Opinion of the Court." *Susette Kelo, et al., Petitioners v. City of New London, Connecticut, et al.* 545 U.S., No. 04–108. June 23, 2005.

Stevens, Stan. Introduction to *Conservation through Cultural Survival: Indigenous Peoples and Protected Areas.* Edited by Stan Stevens. Washington, DC: Island, 1997. 1–8.

———. "The Legacy of Yellowstone." In *Conservation through Cultural Survival: Indigenous Peoples and Protected Areas.* Edited by Stan Stevens. Washington, DC: Island, 1997. 13–32.

———. "New Alliances for Conservation." In *Conservation through Cultural Survival: Indigenous Peoples and Protected Areas.* Edited by Stan Stevens. Washington, DC: Island, 1997. 33–62.

Stowe, Stacey. "Rell Seeks Legislative Review of Ruling on Eminent Domain." *New York Times.* June 25, 2005.

Straw, Richard A., and H. Tyler Blethen. *High Mountains Rising: Appalachia in Time and Place.* Urbana: University of Illinois Press, 2004.

"3 US Judges Hear Park Case Today: Validity of Land Condemnation Act Will Be Argued in Federal Court." *Daily News-Record* (Harrisonburg, VA). December 10, 1934.

Turner, William H., and Edward J. Cabbell, eds. *Blacks in Appalachia.* Lexington: University Press of Kentucky, 1985.

Unrau, Harlan D., and G. Frank Williss. *Administrative History: Expansion of the National Park Service in the 1930s.* Denver: National Park Service, 1983.

"U.S. Will Move Village Where Soap Is Unknown and Chaucer English Is Spoken." *Washington Herald.* May 2, 1932.

Weil, Elsie. "'Lost' Communities in Blue Ridge Hills: Centres Where Intelligence Practically Is Missing Reported by Psychologists." *New York Times.* October 19, 1930.

Whisnant, Anne Mitchell. *Super-Scenic Motorway: A Blue Ridge Parkway History.* Chapel Hill: University of North Carolina Press, 2006.

Whisnant, David. *All That Is Native and Fine: The Politics of Culture in an American Region.* Chapel Hill: University of North Carolina Press, 1983.

Wilhelm, Gene. "Folk Culture History of the Blue Ridge Mountains." *Appalachian Journal,* Spring 1975, 192–222.

———. "Shenandoah Resettlements." *Pioneer American,* March 1982, 15–40.

Williams, John Alexander. *Appalachia: A History.* Chapel Hill: University of North Carolina Press, 2001.

Wine, Daniel P., and Harold E. Phillips. *Shenandoah National Park: Official Pictorial Book.* Harrisonburg, VA: Shenandoah National Park Tourist Bureau, 1929.

Wolfram, Walt, and Donna Christian. *Appalachian Speech.* Washington, DC: Center for Applied Linguistics, 1976.

Wyatt-Brown, Betram. *The Shaping of Southern Culture: Honor, Grace and War, 1760's–1880's.* Chapel Hill: University of North Carolina Press, 2001.

Index

Italicized page numbers refer to illustrations.